Table of Contents

BACK TO BASICS

Published by HAYES PRESS

The Barn, Flaxlands,

Royal Wootton Bassett,

Swindon

UK SN4 8DY

t. +44 (0)1793 850598

e. info@hayespress.org

www.hayespress.org

www.facebook.com/hayespress.org

http://twitter.com/#!/hayespress

British Library Cataloguing Data

A catalogue of this title is available from the British Library.

Printed in the UK 2014

Foreword

Our title, notwithstanding its fairly recent and somewhat discredited use as a political slogan in the United Kingdom, plainly states what we are about. We could have avoided any negative association, and remained alliterative, by employing some such alternative as Apostolic Absolutes; Biblical Basics; Core Convictions; Distinctive Doctrines; Evangelical Essentials; Faith's Fundamentals ... we could probably go through the alphabet! However, as a title, what we have serves us well enough. The Bible has generated a vast wealth of sermons, and various published 'Systematic Theologies' attempt to quite exhaustively catalogue very many doctrinal assertions. The eager Bible student will scan these with some profit, but at some point the question will arise: 'What are the key elements which are characteristic of, and defining for, Christianity?' Also, 'What are the main points of first importance practically which I should focus on so as to live to please the Lord?'

In answer to that, this is a book which examines the core beliefs essential to the Christian faith - why we believe what we do about God, the Bible, the cross and the Apostolic Faith central to New Testament Christianity. Each of the chapters first appeared as an article in the NT magazine published by the Churches of God (see http://churchesofgod.info/media/publications/#NeededTruth).
Readers found them a helpful summary of the things which are sincerely believed by us, and so we commend this compilation as a handy resource. Please have your Bible open as you enjoy going through it!

TABLE OF CONTENTS

Foreword

Epilogue

CHAPTER ONE: THE TRINITY (DAVID VILES)

The Fundamental of Fundamentals

Although defined as 'the central dogma of Christian theology',[1] the term Trinity is nowhere explicitly stated in Scripture. Rather, it is a sublime concept, progressively revealed by God in His Word, which is nevertheless capable of deduction and acceptance by the finite minds of humankind. A classic description is 'one God subsisting in three persons and one substance'. The words 'persons' and 'substance' are highly specific in this context – we will return to them later.

Whatever the Trinity means, it must therefore be fundamental to understanding who God is and what God does. The figures one and three are crucial to such understanding. Christianity will emphatically concur with the Jew that 'the Lord our God is one Lord',[2] but will add that He subsists in three Persons. This fundamental qualification accounts for the continuing opposition of Judaism to Christianity, ever since the Son of God declared, *"I and the Father are one."*[3] It also places Christianity at complete odds with Moslem monotheism.[4]

This may already seem remote and complex, but the implications are also fundamental in a much more human way. For John to declare that 'God is love'[5] has little real meaning unless God had somebody to love before He created mankind in His own image – love involves at least two persons. Jesus insisted that the Father loves the Son with absolute candour and unity of purpose.[6] This sublime love, subsisting and streaming eternally between the Persons of the Trinity, is presented to us as the fount of all human love.[7]

Explaining the Trinity – Principles

Basic as this doctrine is, it has never ceased to be controversial. For some people, the intellectual difficulty of encompassing a God who is both one and three, is enough for the Trinity to be relegated to the theological back burner or even rejected. There are therefore some basic principles by which the disciple will wish to be guided:

1. We are used to complexity, both in our everyday lives and in the creation around us. Can we expect the Creator – immortal, living in light unapproachable, majestic in holiness – to be any more accessible to our finite minds?

2. The Trinity, like all of Scripture, is the product of divine revelation, and God knows how much revelation we can endure of His ineffable glory. There are *secret things* which belong only to Him, and surely the fullness of the relationships within the Trinity is one of these. Nevertheless, *the things revealed belong to us*[8] – assuring us that the Spirit will use meditation on these high and holy revelations to enrich our spiritual lives

3. There are limitations imposed by our human condition in considering the nature and character of God. One is language, by which God has chosen to reveal Himself, but which is nevertheless inadequate to the task of communicating His reality. We therefore need to be very careful about the words that we use, recognising their limitations.

Another limitation is our environment, particularly our domination by time. We are driven to use analogies in seeking to explain and defend the Trinity. There is nothing wrong with this approach, provided we are sensitive to the limitations implicit in comparing a thing or a state with the eternal and limitless. For example, in describing the unity and diversity of the Trinity we may choose the analogy of a man who is at once a husband, father and son, uniting three different functions in one person. This is helpful as far as it goes, but it fails to do full justice to the relationships within the Trinity which demand equality and universality as well as diversity.[2]

So, confronted by these ineffable facts about God, the humble disciple can only wonder and adore, being content to accept the Trinity as a doctrine which accommodates all the relevant Scriptural revelation. The process thereafter of pursuing analogies which go some way towards explaining it in human terms is legitimate, but to proceed the other way – fitting the doctrine into an allegorical system – is likely to skew and oversimplify any attempt to understand the revealed nature of God.

A Little History ...

One important example of an unbalanced approach to the Trinity is afforded by the Arian controversy of the fourth century. Arius (c.250-336) taught that Christ, though creator and redeemer, was not of one substance with the Father, being born in time. The root of his error lay precisely in over-emphasising selective Scriptures at the expense of the whole revelation, considering the eternal truths of Christ's divine nature through the perspective of space and time, and in failing to acknowledge the limitations of language in expressing this divine nature.

John repeatedly describes the Son as being *"the only begotten of the Father".*[10] Arius interpreted this, in conjunction with certain Scriptures implying order in the Trinity,[11] in a space/time context so as to indicate that Christ was willed into existence by God. A similar stumbling block was provided by the Greek word '*hupostasis*' in the context of Hebrews 1:3 – the *'image of his substance'* (RV) in relation to the nature of Christ. Here is a material word – meaning basis or foundation – used by the Spirit-guided writer in a highly technical, theological sense.[12] Arians argued that the Son was not of the same substance, but of a like substance, with the Father, again suggesting that the Son is inferior.

So serious were the implications of this teaching, that a Council was held at Nicea in 325, resulting in the famous credal formulation describing the Son as 'begotten not made, being of one substance with the Father'. A later Council described the Spirit as 'the Lord. ... who proceeds from the Father and the Son and with the Father and the Son together is worshipped and glorified.' These classic formulations have stood the test of time, because they take account of the full Scriptural revelation about the Trinity – particularly those which emphasise the eternal existence of the Son in equality with the Father[13] and the divine nature of the Lord the Spirit.[14]

These remote debates continue to resonate today. Arian interpretations of monotheism are still propounded by various unitarian groups and by sects such as the Jehovah's Witnesses. And the Nicean debates still leave some loose ends, such as the use of the word 'Person' to describe the Trinity. This word requires cautious use in this context – in the normal sense 'persons' signifies individuals with different knowledge, feelings and will. But in the theological sense, these qualities are all identical.[15]

What is God – One in Three

There are many instances, some already referred to [13] [14], which make clear the divine nature of the Son and the Spirit, both sharing the attributes of the Father. One particularly noteworthy example is the Great Commission,[15] where the risen Lord enjoins the disciples to baptise in one name – God – but in all three Persons.

It will have been noted that nearly all the references above are to the New Testament, but it is clear that the Trinity is also at work before the incarnation. Even in the uncompromising monotheism of Deutoronomy 6:4, the word *'echad'* describes 'one' God not in isolation but one in unity, for example as in a bunch of grapes or one people. Turning to the New Testament, it is unsurprising that the work of the Trinity is particularly evident during the 'days of his flesh' – in Christ's incarnation,[16] baptism[17] and resurrection[18] and in the act of atonement.[19]

However, focusing on the essential unity of will and work implicit in the Trinity is only part of the story and can, again, skew our understanding of this sublime truth. Before even Arius, the Sabellians taught that Father, Son and Spirit were only temporary manifestations of the one God, assumed for the purpose of redemption. This error has the apparent virtue of 'simplicity' and is therefore still alive today, but it fails to do justice to the Scriptural revelation of diversity in the Trinity, to which we now turn.

Who is God – Three in One

One of the most beautiful and comforting of Scriptures is surely the apostolic blessing.[20] This indicates that we are right to discern a diversity of function in the Trinity – in this case, all directed towards us! Other Scriptures point us towards distinctive focuses of the work of each Person[21] and in specific areas – such as creation[22] – particular functions are very evident. Ascribing set roles to each Person (modalism), by which God as Father provides and creates, while in His role as Son He redeems and lives in believers in the mode of the Spirit, is far too restrictive. For example, there are aspects by which all three Persons abide within the heart of the believer.[23]

So where do we conclude? While recognising that the Trinity is not to be pigeonholed by our puny minds, we may safely summarise that God reveals Himself to us as God above,[24] God beside[25] and God within[26] and that these are particular (but not exclusive) focuses of the respective Persons of the Trinity.

[1] The Oxford Dictionary of the Christian Church; [2] Deut.6:4 RV; [3] John 10:30; [4] "Do not speak of a Trinity ... God is only one God, He is far above having a Son." Qu'ran 4:171; [5] 1 John 4:8; [6] John 3:35; 5:20, cf. Col.1:13; [7] 1 John 4:7- 21; [8] Deut.29:29; [9] John 1:1; 1 Cor.2:10-11; [10] John 1:14,18 RV ; [11] Such as John 14:28 and 1 Cor.8:5-6. That there is order in the Trinity is clear (*"The Father is greater than I"*) but, taken with other Scriptures, it is also clear that this does not imply inferiority; [12] The difficulties of rendering this word in a way which is meaningful is demonstrated by the variety of English translations. [13] e.g. John 10:30 (*"I and the Father are one"*): John 1:1; Col. 2:9 (*All the fullness of the Deity*); [14] e.g. Ps. 139:7; 1 Cor. 2:10-12; Jn.14:16 RV (*"another Comforter"*, lit. *"another of the same kind"*); Acts 5:1-4; [15] Matt.28:18-20; [16] Luke 1:35; [17] Luke 3:21-22; [18] John 10:17-18; Rom.6:4; 8:11; [19] Heb.9:14; [20] *May the grace of the Lord Jesus Christ, and the love of God, and the fellowship of the Holy Spirit be with you all* (2 Cor.13:14); [21] e.g. Jude 20-21; [22] Gen.1:1-2; John 1:3; [23] 1 John 4:13-15; John 14:23; 2 Cor.1:21-22; [24] Gen. 1:1-3; [25] Matt. 1:23; 28:20; [26] John 14:15-18; Acts 1:8

Bible quotations from the NIV unless otherwise stated.

CHAPTER TWO: GOD IN MY LIFE: MY RELATIONSHIP WITH THE TRINITY (KARL SMITH)

God doesn't intend us to know about Him; He intends us to know Him. This is true not only about God as a total, single Being, but also about each of three Persons that express His unique identity. Speaking to the 'Father', the Lord Jesus said that it was possible for human beings to *"know you the only true God, and Jesus Christ whom you have sent"*.[1] After the Spirit had been given, John went on to write that it was equally possible to *know the Spirit of God*.[2] Of course when one is present, all are present, because God is One and indivisible. Our relationship with God, however, is intended to be so real that we can know them individually and recognize the distinctive character of their work within the total work of God.

The Father

When we speak of God as 'The Father', we mean that He is the Father of the Lord Jesus. More than this, however, the risen Christ spoke of Him as *"my Father and your Father"*.[3] If we have had a father with a loving, protective, teaching and generous nature, we can readily identify with God on these terms.

We have the privilege of speaking to God the Father directly: *"In that day you will ask in my name, and I do not say to you that I will ask the Father on your behalf; for the Father himself loves you."*[4] In our normal prayer, especially in worship or making requests, we address our words *in the Holy Spirit*[5] to the Father in the name of the Lord Jesus. We come as a child to a Father, recognizing Him respectfully as the

11

authoritative head of the family, but also seeing His affectionate care for our development. He said of one of Israel's tribes, *"it was I who taught Ephraim to walk; I took them up by their arms"*[6] and the same is true for us. The Lord Jesus points to the gifts that fathers give to their children and asks, *"how much more will your Father who is in heaven give good things to those who ask him!"*[7] We can ask in confidence that, if it's good for us, He will give it to us. I wish I knew more of this confidence in prayer and of this simple relationship with God as a son to a loving Father.

The Son

The Lord Jesus uses many paired words to describe our relationship to Himself. These include the shepherd and the sheep,[8] the vine and the branches[9] and the lord and the servant.[10] All of these are useful, but among them all, I find myself thinking daily of our relationship as that of master and disciple. Our goal is summed up in Luke 6:40: *"A disciple is not above his teacher, but everyone when he is fully trained will be like his teacher."*

The disciples learned from their master not just from what He said, but also from being with Him almost every day, doing ordinary everyday things. They saw how He responded to the little things in life that irritate us all and watched what brought a smile to the face of this Man of Sorrows. They learned His values and got to know His way by getting to know Him. I am finding more and more in my quiet times that when I read the Gospel narratives or teaching, I picture myself as His disciple waiting to see what He is going to do or listening to hear what He has to say. If the passage is from the Old Testament, I look for things that point to the need for His coming or that predict His appearance. I picture myself walking on the Emmaus road with Him as, *"beginning with Moses and all the Prophets, he interpreted to them in all the Scriptures the things concerning himself*.[11] Even if I don't see the relevance immediately, I can file it away until such time as in study or meditation, *"His disciples remembered that it was written..."*[12] The epistles and Revelation brim over with information about Him.

Sometimes I repeat the verses that speak about Himself. In this way I enjoy communion with Him around the things that are written about Him. Believe me, it makes it harder to skim over His sufferings or indeed His commandments. You can get a clear sense of the Master's instructions and nothing adds a sense of purpose to your day like that. Best of all, it helps in the process of getting to know Him personally, for He is a living person.

The Spirit

There's a temptation for people of my generation to think of the Holy Spirit as something like the Force in *Star Wars*, something vaguely out there to be channeled and used by the disciple of the Lord. Actually it's the other way round. He is a highly personal presence and we are there to be used by Him.

I am most conscious of the leading of the Holy Spirit when I have been in committee meetings with people dedicated to some aspect of God's work. Some problem that seemed impossible to resolve before the meeting began has come up, the Lord's help has been asked for and a way forward has emerged that can be agreed on. Or perhaps we are looking for direction about a particular aspect of the work and all we have to begin with is a blank sheet of paper. Then it appears that several people have been thinking the same thought totally independently of each other. We take this and talk it through and suddenly we're aware that the solution seems to fit the need to be addressed exactly.

At this point in the discussion, you recognize that the Holy Spirit has been moving through the room, invited at the beginning, but barely noticed. His presence is familiar from similar leading at various points in your life and the character of His leading is consistent and recognizably His: "*The wind blows where it wishes, and you hear its sound, but you do not know where it comes from or where it goes. So it is with everyone who is born of the Spirit.*"[13]

Like electricity or the wind, the Spirit Himself is invisible, but His existence can be seen clearly in the effects He produces in the lives of disciples. He prefers to deflect the glory to Christ, as the Lord Jesus' words make clear: "*He will glorify me, for he will take what is mine and declare it to you.*"[14]

The familiar blessing from 2 Corinthians 13:14, "*The grace of the Lord Jesus Christ and the love of God and the fellowship of the Holy Spirit be with you all*", shows how Father, Son and Spirit act together and cannot be separated, but our spiritual experience is enriched by recognizing the distinct notes in the three-part harmony of God's indivisible work.

[1] John 17:3; [2] 1 John 4:2; [3] John 20:17; [4] John 16:26-7; [5] Jude 20; [6] Hos.11:3; [7] Matt.7:11; [8] e.g. John 10; [9] John 15; [10] e.g. Matt.25:21 NKJV; [11] Luke 24:27; [12] John 2:17; [13] John 3:8; [14] John 16:14

Bible quotations are from the ESV.

CHAPTER THREE: BY FAITH ALONE: ETERNALLY SECURE SALVATION (CRAIG JONES)

It has been reported on a Christian news website[1] that, in January 2009, Pope Benedict declared that Martin Luther was right after all and that one of the rallying cries of the Reformation of the 16th century, *sola fide* (by faith alone), was indeed a correct understanding of biblical truth. Together with *sola scriptura* (by scripture alone) and *sola gratia* (by grace alone), these 'soundbites' distil the main tenets of the Reformation movement that led to the establishment of Protestantism, from which we can trace most non-Catholic western Christian denominations in existence today.

It all goes back to 1517, when a Catholic monk, Martin Luther, posted written objections to certain Roman Catholic teachings concerned with forgiveness and eternal salvation, on the door of a church in Wittenberg, Germany. Luther became convinced that forgiveness and salvation are granted to the individual only through the saving grace of God, on the basis solely of their faith in the redeeming work of Christ on the cross, as clearly taught in the Bible and perhaps most succinctly captured in Ephesians 2:8-9: "*For by grace you have been saved through faith; and that not of yourselves, it is the gift of God; not as a result of works, so that no one may boast.*" Up to that time, the prevailing understanding and teaching of the Roman Catholic church was (and indeed still is) that salvation, forgiveness and eternal life, although deriving from the grace of God, can only be made sure by people on the basis of faithful adherence to various practices and sacraments – in other words, 'works'.

And so today, we basically have these two branches of 'Christianity'; one which holds to a 'works-based' doctrine of salvation and the other which maintains a 'faith-only' doctrine. However, even within the 'faith-only' branch, there are differences of understanding in regard to salvation. One view holds that once saved by faith alone according to the grace of God, the believer can never lose his salvation, regardless of what he subsequently does in life. The other view, however, teaches 'conditional security' – that whilst salvation is indeed granted on the basis of God's grace through faith alone, unless believers remain faithful throughout their lives, their salvation can be lost, they can become 'unsaved'.

This is probably thought to be most clearly illustrated from Galatians 5:4, *"You have been severed from Christ, you who are seeking to be justified by law; you have fallen from grace."* Paul seems to be declaring that believers in the Lord Jesus, by backsliding into un-Christian beliefs and practices from which they were initially delivered, can lose their position in God's grace, hence their salvation. In order to avoid this then, it seems we must ensure we are always doing things that we believe demonstrate our faith. The burden of proof, therefore, is effectively on the individual believer.

The thrust of New Testament teaching concerning the new covenant consistently contrasts the failure of mankind to keep the law in order to attain salvation with the free grace and righteousness available through repentance and personal faith in the Lord Jesus. The inevitable consequence of this is that ultimate salvation cannot be assured (since our sinful nature is still active, constantly tempting us away from our faith) and becomes, at best, based on the efforts and merits of the individual believer. Is this really consistent with the thrust of New Testament teaching (e.g. Romans and Hebrews especially) concerning the new covenant, which consistently contrasts the failure of mankind to keep the law in order to attain salvation, with the free grace and righteousness available through repentance and personal faith in the Lord Jesus? Is there another way that can we understand Galatians 5:4 that **is** consistent with New Testament teaching?

The word translated 'severed' is more often rendered 'nullify' in other verses in the New Testament. It literally means 'made useless' and so puts a different complexion on Galatians 5:4. When we allow ourselves to fall back into a life of sin, of negligence towards what the Lord has called us to be and do, then we can become useless to Him and His purposes. He is no longer able to use us in His service and we lose out on the joy and delight of that experience.

The Lord Himself also spoke of this in John 15:6, where those who do not maintain a close, living, dynamic relationship with Him (the 'true vine'), risk becoming withered and useless, bearing no fruit. This is also the sense of Philippians 2:12, where Paul encourages us to *work out your salvation* – not to 'figure out how by your own effort you can become saved', but 'in the state of being saved, work for the Lord to the end'.

There are many scriptures which state clearly that saving faith is a 'one-off' act, and that, from that moment on, Christian believers are eternally secure in their salvation. For example, Ephesians 1:13-14 confirms to us that the Holy Spirit indwells us at the moment of our salvation (expressed in the past tense) and that the fact of His indwelling is the 'pledge' or 'guarantee' of our future, heavenly inheritance.

In John 5:24, the Lord declares, *"Truly, truly, I say to you, he who hears My word, and believes Him who sent Me, has eternal life, and does not come into judgment, but has passed out of death into life"*. Whilst 'conditional security' proponents would highlight the continuous present tense of 'hears' and 'believes' in this verse, the passing from death to life is a definite one-off, past action. Romans 11:29 declares that 'the gifts and the calling of God are irrevocable', so we are assured about the 'once-for-all' nature of saving faith.

Is it possible to then come back under condemnation and death? Paul categorically tells us, *"Therefore there is now no condemnation for those who are in Christ Jesus. For the law of the Spirit of life in Christ Jesus has set you free* [i.e. a completed, past action] *from the law of sin and of death."*[2] Then we have those wonderful words from the Lord in John 10:28-29 *"... and they shall never perish; and no one shall snatch them out of My hand. My Father, who has given them to Me ... no one is able to snatch them out of the Father's hand,"* where we again see the confirmation of a one-off, past, complete action of the Father in securing to the Lord those who have believed in Him.

From Ephesians 2:8-9 we understand that salvation is *'the gift of God'* by grace and through faith; and when we link that with Romans 11:29, which declares that *"the gifts and the calling of God are irrevocable"*, we are further assured about the 'once-for-all' nature of saving faith.

One of the main issues that conditional security adherents have with this truth about eternal security, is that it allows for – perhaps even encourages – the attitude that, "I don't need to actually live like a Christian because I know I'm saved anyway," and that it fosters indifference towards ongoing sin in the believer's life, giving licence for indulgence in sin.

Paul understood that possibility very well and addressed it in Romans 6, declaring twice, *"May it never be!"* In chapter 7:4, he then shows that salvation is not an end in itself, but that we are indeed saved for a purpose: *"in order that we might bear fruit for God"*. This fruit is to be expressed through our diligent obedience to what the Lord has called us to in salvation, so that we should continue in the *"good works, which God prepared beforehand so that we would walk in them"*[3] because, as he further explains, as believers *"we must all appear before the judgment seat of Christ, so that each one may be recompensed for his deeds in the body, according to what he has done, whether good or bad"* [4] – not judgement of sin, but of our service for Him.

[1]   http://au.christiantoday.com/article/luther-rome-and-the-bible/5255.htm; [2] Rom.8:1-2; [3] Eph.2:10 [4] 2 Cor.5:10

Bible quotations from the NASB.

CHAPTER FOUR: TAKING HOLD – WHAT AM I DOING WITH MY ETERNAL LIFE? (RICHARD HUTCHINSON)

Paul encouraged Timothy to "*take hold of the eternal life to which [he was] called*".[1] Timothy had laboured alongside Paul in his missionary journeys and Paul was entrusting the care of the church in Ephesus and the fight against false teachers in that area to this young man; yet Paul urged such an active and obviously spiritually mature disciple to *take hold* of his eternal life. Surely, then, this is a message for all disciples. Have we not taken hold of what the Lord has won for us at such a high price? Have we missed out on the fullness of God's blessing to us through the Lord Jesus by simply not reaching out and taking hold of it?

Our belief in the Lord Jesus has not only dealt with the penalty for our sins, but it has opened up the possibility of living in the here and now *"that which is truly life"*,[2] a phrase that calls to mind how the Lord told the Pharisees that He had come that *"they may have life and that they may have it more abundantly"*.[3] We have an eternal life through faith that guarantees an eternity in God's presence. However, if we are reserving consideration of our eternal life for that future glory, like a token for access to heaven that we keep tucked away in our pocket, we are neglecting a significant part of what the Lord achieved for us through the cross. We must take hold of it and make it real every day.

How Do We 'Take Hold'?

Paul tells the disunited church in Philippi to *"work out your own salvation."*[4] This is not, of course, anything to do with justification by works, but an exhortation to be working at what has been given to us. Our salvation from sin's penalty is once for all, but our salvation from its power over our day-to-day lives is an ongoing concern. The Greek word *'katergazomai'* used for 'work out' implies finishing something already begun; fashioning something – as if salvation in this sense is like a lump of clay needing to be shaped. Earlier in his epistle, Paul had told the Philippians that God would perfect the work He had begun in them,[5] and now going deeper, he tells them to work their salvation like a potter works his clay, or a carpenter works the wood.

It may seem contradictory, but not when read with the reassurance that follows it: *"it is God who works in you."*[6] One fashions an object with a final state in mind, and so it is with God, who seeks our co-operation in bringing us to a likeness of His Son.[7] To fashion a thing, one must first take hold of it, and we must actively, consciously work at applying the reality of being a new creation in Christ each day.[8] I have been freed from the power of sin by Christ's sacrifice on my behalf, for example, but did my life today prove that to be a reality? I have a sure and certain hope of the Lord's return based on God's promise, but did that functionally affect how I acted at any point today? I have a constant spring of joy and peace in my heart because of my reconciled position with God, but did I at any point draw from it today to countermand the frustrations and disappointments that beset me?

He Also Laid Hold of Me

Paul admitted that he was still striving to do this very same thing. *"Not that I have already attained* [lit. 'taken hold'] *or am already perfected, but I press on, that I may lay hold of that for which Christ Jesus has also laid hold of me.*[2]

The Lord took hold of you when He saved you. He took hold of you and pulled you out of the mire of sin; He took hold of you and pulled you up on your feet to walk with Him in discipleship; He took hold of you and lifted you up to sit in the heavenly places with Him.[10] He took hold of you so that you could take hold of a true and eternal life that would yield *'joy and peace in believing'.*[11] Therefore let us take hold with both hands daily and fashion it a little more each day for the glory of the grace of our God.

[1] 1 Tim.6:12 ; [2] 1 Tim.6:19; [3] John 10:10 NKJV; [4] Phil.2:12; [5] Phil.1:6; [6] Phil.2:13; [7] Rom.8:29; [8] 2 Cor.5:15-17; [9] Phil.3:12 NKJV; [10] Eph.2:6; [11] Rom.15:13

Bible quotations from the ESV unless stated otherwise.

CHAPTER FIVE: IN THE WATER – BAPTISM OF BELIEVERS (ALEX REID)

All Christians agree that the medium of physical baptism should be water. However, they are not unanimous about how the ordinance should be carried out. All of the following modes are practised: sprinkling with water, pouring water upon, or complete immersion in water.

Firstly, we need to grasp the meaning of the original Greek word for baptism. W.E. Vine says, *Baptizo: to baptize, primarily a frequentative form of bapto, to dip, was used among the Greeks to signify the dyeing of a garment, or the drawing of water by dipping a vessel into another, etc.*[1] The thought, then, is dipping into, not sprinkling or pouring upon.

Secondly, the New Testament descriptions of baptism portray the one being baptised as going down into and coming up out of the water. For example, *"Jesus came from Nazareth in Galilee and was baptized by John in the Jordan. Immediately coming up out of the water, He saw the heavens opening".*[2] Also, in Acts 8:38, *"they both went down into the water, Philip as well as the eunuch, and he baptized him. When they came up out of the water, the Spirit of the Lord snatched Philip away."*

Thirdly, the Scriptures tell us what baptism is meant to symbolize: *"Therefore we have been buried with Him through baptism into death, so that as Christ was raised from the dead through the glory of the Father, so we too might walk in newness of life. For if we have become united with Him in the likeness of His death, certainly we shall also be in the likeness of His resurrection."*[3] Only baptism by immersion is consistent with the symbol of death and resurrection.

Opponents of immersion may try to dispute the impact of these individual points, but, when combined, they show that immersion is the only mode that fully meets New Testament criteria for the ordinance of baptism.

Whom Should We Baptise?

Answers to this question fall into two main groupings; those who would baptise infants, usually by sprinkling or pouring, and those who would baptise only those professing faith in Christ, usually by immersion, generally called believer's baptism. Those who would sanction the baptism of infants lay emphasis on the faith of the parents or godparents who put the child forward for baptism; whereas with believer's baptism it is the faith of the individual seeking baptism that is emphasised.

There is no record in the New Testament of infants being baptised. Those who would argue such a case suggest that there must have been children among the household members mentioned in Acts 10:24,48 and 16:31,33 at the conversions of Cornelius and the jailer of Philippi respectively, and in the household of Stephanas mentioned in 1 Corinthians 1:16. This is a very weak argument as it rests on supposition rather than stated fact. Moreover, 1 Corinthians 16:15-17 indicates that the 'household' of Stephanas were adult enough to devote themselves in Christian service, and in the other instances it is evident that all who were baptised had the capacity to listen to preaching and respond.[4]

Another line of argument adopted in support of baptising children is one which argues from analogy. For example, from 1 Corinthians 10:1-2 it is argued that there must have been infants among the people of Israel who were all baptised into Moses in the cloud and in the sea, therefore infants can be baptized. Although analogies are often useful in illustrating a point, they can mislead and are not solid ground on which to base an argument. There is not much logic in this analogy: it is only people who are capable of making a rational decision who are to be baptised. Otherwise, what about Israel's flocks and herds?

The above arguments plus others are used to try to justify infant baptism, but in Acts 2:41 it is stated: "*So then, those who had received his word* [Peter's preaching of Christ] *were baptized*". The same pattern of belief first, then baptism, is repeated in the case of the Ethiopian eunuch of Acts 8:34-39; of the centurion Cornelius of Acts 10 and the jailer of Philippi in Acts 16:31-34. In all these cases personal faith in Christ was exercised by the individual concerned before being baptised, something that could not be expected of a babe in arms.

Is Baptism Necessary for Salvation?

Certain scriptures are put forward to support the idea that baptism is a necessary act in receiving eternal salvation, and we shall deal with some of them shortly. First we need to establish an important principle: the New Testament clearly teaches that the forgiveness of sins and eternal life are obtained through faith alone. The following references should be sufficient to establish the point: John 1:12; 5:24; Acts 10:43; 16:31; Romans 1:16-17; 5:1; 10:9 and Ephesians 2:8-9. If personal salvation from the penalty of sin is the product of faith alone, then any scripture linking baptism and salvation must be either an exceptional case - or refer to a different aspect of salvation. The closest thing we have to an explanation of baptism is found in 1 Peter 3:20-21:

> "*The patience of God kept waiting in the days of Noah, during the construction of the ark, in which a few, that is, eight persons, were brought safely through the water* [or 'were saved through water' NKJV]. *Corresponding to that, baptism now saves you – not the removal of dirt from the flesh, but an appeal*

to God for a good conscience – through the resurrection of Jesus Christ.

When reading verses that use the words 'saved' or 'salvation', it is always a sound idea to ask, saved from what? The water, if understood as the means of salvation here, did not deliver Noah from judgement (which was the function of the ark), but delivered him and his family from the evil generation among whom they had lived. Likewise a believer in his or her baptism is declaring that he has died to sin and is beginning to walk in newness of life[5] on the basis of a good conscience towards God which acts to deliver him or her from former sinful associations.

There are other verses that are often put forward in an attempt to support the contention that baptism is necessary for eternal salvation. For example, *"He who has believed and has been baptized shall be saved."*[6] This verse might be understood in the light of what has been said above: that belief or faith alone delivers from the penalty of sin, and baptism is a declaration of intent that we should be delivered from a worldly way of life. Or certainly it could be pointed out (from the continuation of the same verse: *"he who has disbelieved shall be condemned"*) that disbelief alone results in condemnation, which indicates that belief alone brings salvation, and baptism is the public confession of that true faith.

"Now why do you delay? Get up and be baptized, and wash away your sins, calling on His name."[7] This is a verse often quoted in support of the idea of baptismal regeneration, which teaches that baptism is the means of spiritual rebirth. In the light of other scriptures that clearly teach the cleansing from sin through the blood of Christ,[8] it is necessary to understand this invitation to the newly converted Saul as an exhortation to put away his former manner of life and to take up the task for which the Lord had called him.

"Peter said to them, 'Repent, and each of you be baptized in the name of Jesus Christ for the forgiveness of your sins"[2] would seem to be the exception to the line of exposition followed so far, and so needs to be understood in the context in which it was spoken. These words were proclaimed on the day of Pentecost, in the city of Jerusalem, to the same populace that a few weeks previously had bayed for the blood of the Lord. Theirs ('the house of Israel', v.36) was a special culpability in the condemning to death of the Son of God. From them, therefore, an exceptional test was required; namely, that to experience forgiveness of sin they must not only repent and believe in Jesus as the Christ, but also make a very public acknowledgement of their commitment to Jesus Christ as their Lord and master.

Conclusion

The teaching of the New Testament is that believers in Jesus Christ should be baptised by immersion in water as a symbol of what has already happened to them spiritually and as a public declaration that they are followers of the Lord Jesus, and as such have put away their former manner of life.

[1] Vine's Expository Dictionary of Old & New Testament Words; [2] Mark 1:9-10; [3] Rom.6:4-5; [4] Acts 10:44; 16:32,34; [5] see Rom. 6:3-6; [6] Mark 16:16; [7] Acts 22:16; [8] e.g. 1 John 1:7-9; Heb.9:14; [9] Acts 2:38

Bible quotations from the NASB.

CHAPTER SIX: WALKING IN NEWNESS OF LIFE (STEPHEN HICKLING)

Baptisms are always special occasions, but what I particularly like about them is the profound, yet clear, imagery of the believer going down into the water and then being raised out of it. The symbolism of death, burial and resurrection is so plain. You cannot fail to be struck by its powerful testimony to the dramatic event which has already taken place in that believer's life as a result of his placing faith in the Lord Jesus Christ: he has died with Christ to sin and has been made alive in Christ to God!

Baptisms also serve as welcome reminders to those of us who have been baptized of the important commitment we made to the Lord Jesus when we were united with Him in the likeness of His death and resurrection at our own baptism. The very public declaration of our being lifted out of the baptismal waters was that we had already made a new start; and now from this baptismal day until the Lord returns for us, we would walk in newness of life.

> *"Therefore we have been buried with Him through baptism into death, so that as Christ was raised from the dead through the glory of the Father, so we too might walk in newness of life."*[1]

The Reality of the New Life

The language of Romans 6:4 corresponds with the words of the popular chorus,

"I am a new creation,

No more in condemnation

Here in the grace of God I stand."

(Dave Bilbrough)

The 'newness of life' now to be displayed in the walk of the baptized disciple can be expected on the basis that he is already a 'new creation'. *"Therefore, if anyone is in Christ, he is a new creation; old things have passed away; behold, all things have become new."*[2] The change that takes place at the moment of the sinner's conversion is so radical, so complete and so permanent, that the hand of the great Creator is as evident in this work as it was when He first created the heavens and the earth!

The reality of the new birth is that God has not simply repaired or mended us; rather, He has started again and created us anew! The change that takes place at the moment of the sinner's conversion is so radical, so complete and so permanent, that the hand of the great Creator is as evident in this work as it was when He first created the heavens and the earth!

The use of the word 'newness' in Romans 6:4 is emphatic; newness is the prominent theme in the apostle's mind. 'Newness' (and indeed the word for 'new' in 2 Corinthians 5:17) does not simply refer to something that is new in time (i.e. recent or young), but new in quality or character. It implies that this new creation, or life, is completely different in character from anything that existed previously. The old things of the old creation have passed away and have been replaced with new desires, new motives, new principles, new purposes and a new direction. Indeed, for the believer, all things have become new!

In Ephesians 4:24 you find an equivalent expression to the 'new creation' of 2 Corinthians 5: *"the new man which was created according to God, in true righteousness and holiness"*.[3] No wonder this new nature can be described as fresh in quality and character by comparison with what it has replaced: the new man has been created in the likeness of God! By contrast, our old nature (the old man) which was done away with prior to the creation within us of the new nature, takes its likeness from Adam. The old man *"grows corrupt according to the deceitful lusts"*;[4] the new man is continually being *"renewed in knowledge according to the image of Him who created him"*.[5] What a difference!

Interestingly, in Colossians 3:10 the word for 'new' does simply mean new in relation to time. In the context of that verse, it seems to be indicative of the fact that this process of knowledge renewal into the image of the Creator is one which has only just begun. So far as that process, which will engage our eternal lives, is concerned, it's early days for the new man!

Walking – Developing Good Behaviour

Those of us who are parents will be familiar with the happiness that comes from a child taking his or her first steps. For the child, the frustration of those initial wobbles and falls is soon replaced, by repeated practice, with the assurance of balanced technique. The transition from baby to toddler is, of course, a vitally important one for the physical development of a child. It is no less significant in the development of the child of God that he learns to walk, after his spiritual rebirth, in order to experience the fullness of his new life.

W.E. Vine tells us that the word for 'walk' in Romans 6:4 'signifies the whole round of activities of the individual life'.[6] Literally, the word means to walk 'all around'; a very public promenade to display our new-found ability. Walking in the context of Romans 6:4 is all about our behaviour. It's about our showing outwardly (all around) the reality of the change that God has made inwardly at our conversion. At our salvation we received a new spiritual life; at our baptism we publicly declared that we had already died to sin in order that we might thereafter walk in the freshness of that new life.

It would be wrong to think that this matter of walking is something to be mastered by the new Christian and then forgotten. On the contrary, our baptism merely displayed an initial willingness to be subject to the Lord. Is that obedient spirit still recognisable in our present walk? Can others observe in us the evidence of God-given freshness and vitality?

The only other use of the word 'newness' in the New Testament is in the very next chapter of Romans. In a very similar expression to the one we have considered in Romans 6:4, Paul tells us that we *serve in newness of the Spirit and not in oldness of the letter.*[7] Not only has God thoroughly regenerated us, but He has given us the grace by which we might serve Him in keeping with that new life through the enabling power of the Holy Spirit.

What a gracious God we serve! Not only has God thoroughly regenerated us, but He has given us the grace by which we might serve Him in keeping with that new life through the enabling power of the Holy Spirit. The only way it's possible for a newness of walk to be seen in us is because the Spirit makes it so. The contrast: living according to the flesh or walking in newness of life.

When you consider the magnitude of the change that God has made in the believer, you quickly realise that it's simply unthinkable for him to continue to lead a life dominated by sin. Yet, Paul's exhortation in Romans 6:12 implies that this remains a real possibility for the believer: *"Do not let sin reign in your mortal body."* Paul tells the Colossian saints that they *"laid aside the old self with its evil practices, and have put on the new self."*[8] These verses tell of the reality of the divine work in believers on the Lord Jesus. This is the eternal perspective.

The problem is that, whilst in the body, we have still to contend with the old self, which resides there. That's the present struggle that Paul refers to when he addresses the Ephesian saints in regard to their conduct. *"[You] have been taught by Him ... that you put off, concerning your former conduct, the old man which grows corrupt according to the deceitful lusts, and be renewed in the spirit of your mind, and that you put on the new man which was created according to God, in true righteousness and holiness."*[2]

The teaching in Ephesians 4 is that we must take positive action, so far as our conduct is concerned, to ensure that our walk evidences what God has established. We have to clothe ourselves with the new man, but that is only possible if we've first taken off the old man. In His grace and patience, God does not compel us in our decision as to how we will walk. But whenever we decide to put off the old, the Spirit is ready to empower a walk characterised by newness of life.

The key to walking daily in newness of life is to have a proper appreciation of our death! Think back to the day of your baptism and recall how you identified yourself with the death of God's Son. We will never experience the fullness and freshness of living with Him until we appreciate that we died with Him.

*"**Knowing this**, that our old self was crucified with Him, in order that our body of sin might be done away with, so that we would no longer be slaves to sin; for he who has died is freed from sin."*[10]

[1] Rom.6:4; [2] 2 Cor.5:17 NKJV; [3] Eph.4:24 NKJV; [4] Eph.4:22 NKJV; [5] Col.3:10, NKJV; [6] Vine's Expository Dictionary of Old & New

Testament Words; [7] Rom.7:6; [8] Col.3:9-10; [9] Eph.4:21-24 NKJV; [10] Rom.6:6-7

Bible quotations from the NASB unless otherwise stated.

CHAPTER SEVEN: BREAKING THE BREAD – THE LORD'S SUPPER (JAMES NEEDHAM)

In the dark hour of His betrayal, the Lord of the Sabbath broke a loaf and issued a command to resonate in the hearts of His disciples throughout the age to come: 'do this in remembrance of Me'.[1]

Today, the remembrance of the Lord Jesus in the breaking of the bread remains the focal point of the service of those who love God. Disciples in churches of God today meet together to break bread on the first day of each week. In this vital, weekly remembrance, some others see similarities with the Jewish Sabbath and claim that, in continuity with the Old Covenant pattern, this collective remembrance should be undertaken every Saturday. Observance of the Sabbath was imperative to God's Old Covenant people, commanded by God as one of the Ten Commandments of Exodus 20. Did the New Testament practice, therefore, change the day for collective weekly devotion, or has Christian practice over the centuries taken us away from Sabbath observance and obedience to God?

The Importance of the Sabbath

The Sabbath had its beginning at the very beginning of time. In six days, God created the heavens and the earth, and on the seventh day He rested in the glory of His finished work. In His rest God found refreshment[2] and He set apart the seventh day, making it holy.[3] Many years passed before manna appeared on the ground to feed the people of God in their wilderness journey. Certainly, faithful men and women had long kept holy the seventh day in honour of what God had declared in Genesis 2, although the Scriptures contain no mention of the weekly

Sabbath until it is confirmed in Exodus 16. In the Law which bound God's people, the seventh day was again sanctified as a collective memorial for the holy nation. Its purpose was that work would cease and rest be granted to all – both rich and poor, servant and master, Israelite and stranger; its expression was found in the people of God together devoting themselves in the thrill of His service in holy assembly to the Lord.[4]

On the seventh day, the people of God both shared God's rest[5] and remembered their own which came in redemption from His hand.[6] By the grace of God, all were to be 'refreshed' in Him, literally 'taking breath' from the toil which sin had brought to the earth.

The New Testament Practice

In the bright and early days which followed the coming of the Holy Spirit, as the gospel spread with fervour and churches of God were established throughout the ancient world, a new practice of weekly remembrance emerged in which disciples of the Lord Jesus met together on the first day of the week[7] to break bread in accordance with the pattern for church practice delivered to them by the apostles in obedience to the Lord's commands.[8] Initially, Jewish Christians would observe 'the Lord's Supper' as an evening event,[9] as the first day of the week began according to the divine calendar at sundown.[10] When Christianity became the official religion of the Roman empire it seems the breaking of the bread eventually moved to the morning of the first day of the Roman week (the word 'supper' signified 'main meal' not necessarily an evening meal).

In this precious gathering, similarities could be seen with the Jewish Sabbath: it was a weekly assembly;[11] a remembrance of a finished work of redemption which affected all creation;[12] and it was something commanded by and for God.[13] As to the Sabbath, it was a shadow, here was the substance which 'is of Christ'.[14]

With a new covenant and a new ordinance came a new day for its observance. On the last day of the week, the Sabbath had been about looking back on a finished work with restful satisfaction. On the first day of the week – the day on which the last enemy was vanquished[15] – the breaking of the bread looks forward through sorrowful remembrance to the glorious hope of all that His work has accomplished, which shall be revealed throughout the eternal ages[16] and was secured by His resurrection on the first day of the week.[17] So we remember a triumphant Saviour, giving God His rightful portion as the very first church activity of our week.

The Sharing in the Rest of God

For all the similarities between the Sabbath and the breaking of the bread, it is in the collective rest of the people of God that the shadow truly finds its substance. The Lord Jesus' claim to lordship of the Sabbath[18] – an outright claim to deity – follows immediately the divine invitation to rest for all those who labour and are heavy laden.[19] 'Rest' in Matthew 11:28 is *anapauo*, the word denoting the once-for-all and eternal refreshment for the weary sinner in laying his heavy burden of sin at the feet of the Saviour. This rest is developed in verse 29 where the word is *anapausis*, signifying an ongoing Sabbath rest for the soul, not in inactivity, but in the satisfaction of sharing His yoke of service and a lifetime learning of Him who is meek and lowly in heart.

As the writer to the Hebrews leads us into a contemplation of collective service, the Holy Spirit presents a third word for 'rest'. In Hebrews 3, the unbelief of Israel is presented as a warning to us: *'So I swore in My wrath, "They shall not enter My rest"'.*[20] The origin of the oath is Psalm 95:11, where the Hebrew word 'rest' is associated with 'abode' or 'resting-place' and is used elsewhere to describe the resting place of God in His house.[21] Guided by the Holy Spirit, the writer to the Hebrews maintains a consistent theme, for the rest of the people of God is *katapausis,* meaning a 'settling down' or 'making an abode'. The only other recorded use of this word in the New Testament is in Acts 7:49 where Stephen cited Isaiah 66 in respect of the rest associated with God's dwelling-place.

The promise remains to God's people to enter into the rest associated with His house,[22] today made up of 'living stones' – baptised disciples built together according to the pattern of divine teaching to form a spiritual house in which God is pleased to dwell.[23] In the breaking of the bread, His people enter through the veil[24] to appear before Him in answer to the Lord's own command in the Upper Room, and to exercise the high privilege of holy priesthood service, offering 'spiritual sacrifices acceptable to God through Jesus Christ'.[25] (Readers desiring more explanation of this truth are invited to make contact as directed in the epilogue.)

By this means we enter into God's rest, in which the substance and purpose of the Sabbath is revealed in all its grace, for the rest of God in Hebrews 3-4 is also *"a Sabbath- rest for the people of God".*[26] Here the Greek word is *sabbatismos* in which the Sabbath-keeping of the Old Covenant blossoms in purpose to the Sabbath-keeping of the New. Matthew 11 speaks of rest for the sinner and rest for the servant; Hebrews 4 presents Sabbath-rest for the people of God who Christ Himself leads in their obedience of faith into God's dwelling to worship Him for His Son, so powerfully portrayed in the loaf and cup.

The Sabbath initially marked a finished creation; our Sabbath-rest now marks a perfect redemption in which God rests once more, perfectly satisfied with the work of Calvary. Again, He calls men to share His rest, no more a shadow of good things to come, but entering into the very presence of God in the sanctuary, a prelude only to the rest which is eternally ours in Christ.

"As *the Sabbath was made for man, and not man for the Sabbath*",[27] so God wants us to enjoy the rest which comes from being in His presence. Here is something crafted to meet man's spiritual need. The 'holy convocation' of Leviticus 23 is not lost, but fulfilled as the purchased and sanctified people of God assemble and ascend, their hearts full, in worship for the person and work of the triune God in creation and, above all, in glorious redemption.

[1] Luke 22:19; [2] Ex.31:17; [3] Gen.2:2-3; [4] Lev.23:3; Is. 58:13-14; [5] Ex.20:11; [6] Deut.5:15; [7] 1 Cor.16:2; [8] Luke 22:19; Acts 1:3; 2:42; 1 Cor.11:23,24; [9] c.f. 1 Cor.11:20; Acts 20:7; [10] Gen.1:5; [11] Lev.23:3; Acts 20:7; [12] Ex.20:11; Deut.5:15; Matt.26:27-28; Rom.8:20-21; [13] Lev.23:3; Heb.10:25; 1 Pet.2:5; [14] Col.2:16-17; [15] 1 Cor.15:26; 2 Tim.1:10 ; [16] Eph.2:7; [17] John 20:1; [18] Matt.12:8; [19] Matt.11:28-29; [20] Heb.3:11; [21] 1 Chron.28:2; Ps.132:8,14; Is.66:1; [22] Heb.4:1; [23] 1 Pet.2:4-5; [24] Heb.10:19-25; [25] 1 Pet.2:5; [26] Heb.4:9 NIV; [27] Mark 2:27

Bible quotes from the NKJV.

CHAPTER EIGHT: BACK TO THE FUTURE: "DO THIS UNTIL I COME" (DON WILLIAMSON)

How often have you heard or even said the phrase "We will never forget"? I'm sure the older you are the more familiar you are with events that have inspired such a phrase. Those who remember the atrocities against the Jewish people in Poland and Germany during the Second World War will apply the phrase to the various memorials for the victims of these death camps. I remember visiting the Vietnam memorial in Washington, D.C. several years ago and the feeling I had in contemplating the death of 58,195 American soldiers – lives taken at the prime of their youth – was an overwhelming feeling of sadness, and my response was silence. A more recent and more personal tragedy was the loss of life at Columbine High School, Colorado, U.S.A. when twelve students and one teacher were killed in the rage of hatred and darkness. Waiting to hear if your son is still alive, or later walking around the memorial and reading quotes from those who lost their lives, brings meaning to 'Never Forgotten'. All of these are remembering the past and give us an awareness of the cost of human failure and sin.

In Remembrance of Me

As we remember events, places, or people we do so from the perspective of our individual knowledge and appreciation. The Lord Jesus gave us these precious words just before going out to the Garden of Gethsemane, *"Do this in remembrance of Me."*[1] He did this expecting that the disciples would think about all of their experiences with Him, and that the years they spent with Him would be seen in the context of the event that was to come in a few hours.

Yes, the symbols that they were to eat and drink were a reminder of the physical presence of the Lord Jesus on earth, but there was going to be much more significance in taking them as the reality of God's glorious salvation would be revealed. We can imagine the feelings of the disciples as they saw the Lord taken away at the hands of an angry mob, the sense of loss, hopes dashed. It would even be more intense as they saw their Master crucified, taken down and placed in a new tomb, which was then sealed by the Roman authorities.[2] But that wasn't the end of the story. As believers in the Lord Jesus Christ, we remember an event different from the ones mentioned earlier. As time goes on April 20, the day of the Columbine massacre, is remembered as a tragedy of the past: our feelings change and we don't give it as much thought. That is just what we are like as people. The children of Israel were to celebrate the Passover feast once a year on the fourteenth day of the first month.[3] Why? God did not want them to forget what He had done for them, and He wanted them to pass it on to their children.

There are many facets to the powerfully appealing words of the Lord as He appeals to us to remember Him. He knew what was going to happen that day and had lived His life to fulfil it. He also knew that He was going to be victorious over sin, death and Satan's power! The full context of the remembrance of the Lord Jesus is in His life, death, resurrection, ascension into heaven, and His coming again. We don't just remember the past, we also anticipate the future.

Proclaiming!

Paul gives us a wonderful picture of God's will for us in his letter to the Corinthian saints, *"For as often as you eat this bread and drink the cup, you proclaim the Lord's death until He comes".*[4] This verse tells us a great deal about our responsibilities and realities. Let us focus on the realities. We are reminded again of the death of the Lord Jesus. The reason that lovely life had to end in such brutal death would have been known to the Corinthians, as Paul explained: *"For the word of the cross is foolishness to those who are perishing, but to us who are being saved it is the power of God."*[5] He further explains to them that they were bought with a price. The death of Christ is not simply an event of history, but one of personal delivery from sin. This verse brings responsibilities: *"For as often as you ..."* Two things come to mind: first is the expression 'as often' and then the personal appeal as 'you'.

The early disciples, being led by the Spirit of God, practised the breaking of bread on the first day of the week.[6] In order for us to fulfil this pattern of the early church, we must 'gather together', an action for which each of us is responsible. If you are not there, the 'you' of verse 26 is missing and the scripture cannot be personally accomplished. Remember the phrase 'never forgotten'. It takes action to implement this; it takes focus and purpose with resolve. Is it your resolve to be faithful and obedient to the command of the Lord? When gathered together with a church of God we are to eat the bread and drink the cup for a particular purpose. It is to 'proclaim'; meaning to announce, declare, promulgate, and make known.[7] This happens by our presence and by our participation in praise and worship. It is part of our witness! What an exciting thought that each week we are coming together in worship and in witness.

Until He Comes

The sadness that I felt at the Vietnam Memorial is in stark contrast to the experience we have each Sunday in our remembrance of the Lord Jesus. Of course, it is a solemn occasion requiring personal reverence as we meet before our God, but we are meeting in the glorious reality of Christ's victory and of His coming back for His Church. Again, two things come to my mind. First we are confronted with the word 'until'.

This is a word of faith and not sight. Peter speaks of mockers that are *saying "Where is the promise of His coming? For ever since the fathers fell asleep, all continues just as it was from the beginning of creation."*[8] Each time we are together to remember the Lord we are performing an act of faith and living out the words 'one time more and one time less'; meaning, of course, that what we do is one time more than the last time, and one time less before He comes for us. Do we face the same mockers today? Maybe not to our face, but as the world moves on with no regard to the Lord's Day, as God is taken out of institutions and the acknowledgment of men, we are to be faithful in our proclaiming of our Lord and Saviour with the resolve to continue 'until He comes'.

As believers in the Lord Jesus, we are to be living in His promises. Promises are personal! When the Lord Jesus died on the cross He died for you and for me. He also gives us a personal promise about His coming: *"If I go and prepare a place for you, I will come again and receive you to Myself, that where I am, there you may be also."*[9] Each week we are to be living in the anticipation of His coming, knowing that God will not repent of His gifts and promises. We could think about all the changes that are taking place in this world and all the signs that point to the imminent coming of the Lord to the air, but I would appeal to you that it was the promise of seeing Christ again that appealed to the disciples. After His resurrection, the Lord revealed Himself to two disciples as they travelled to a village called Emmaus. After listening to the Lord explain to them the things concerning Himself in all the Scriptures, here was their response: *"Were not our hearts burning within us while He was speaking to us on the road, while He was explaining the Scriptures to us?"*[10] He is to be the focus of our hearts. They should overflow as we anticipate the Breaking of Bread – until He comes!

[1] Luke 22:19; [2] Matt.27:64-66; [3] Num.9:5; [4] 1 Cor.11:26; [5] 1 Cor.1:18; [6] Acts 20:7 & 1 Cor.16:2; [7] Thayer's Lexicon; [8] 2 Pet.3:4; [9] John 14:3; [10] Luke 24:32

Bible quotes from the NASB.

CHAPTER NINE: THE BIBLE – ITS COMPOSITION, CANON AND CONSOLIDATION (DAVID VILES)

In the Past God Spoke

These first words of the Epistle to the Hebrews are remarkable. There is no obligation on God to speak – after all, the heavens already declared His omnipotence,[1] His creation eloquently testified to His everlasting power and divinity.[2] Nevertheless, He determined to do so. These opening verses go on to explain how this spoken revelation, supremely and finally uttered in the Person of the incarnate Word,[3] was formerly transmitted through the prophets. The incarnate Word Himself extends this revelation to the whole corpus of the Jewish holy scriptures - the Old Testament (OT) – *"these are the Scriptures that testify about me".*[4]

Turning to the New Testament (NT), we have the specific assurance of the incarnate Word to apprehensive disciples that a prime focus of the Holy Spirit's work is to teach and remind them of all that Christ had said, and would say, to them.[5] It was the original disciples, and the apostle Paul to whom a special revelation was given,[6] who went on to record this material under the Spirit's guidance.

The Composition of the Bible

We can be confident therefore that what we have in both Testaments is truly the word of God and the ultimate revelation of all that we need to know for practical purposes. *"All Scripture"*, says Paul about the OT, *"is God- breathed ... so that the man of God may be thoroughly equipped for every good work.*"[7] And yet the Bible is clearly not a work of dictation. The diverse personalities, fears, preoccupations and ambitions of a wide variety of writers across millennia are reflected and respected, and the whole is far greater than the sum of its parts. There is clear evidence of design, consistency and purpose, with internal corroboration of doctrine, prophecy and historical fact between its component books and across the Testaments. The process of this written revelation is mysterious, and was no doubt intensely personal to those to whom it was given; we are told that *"men spoke from God as they were carried along by the Holy Spirit"*[8] – clearly a process combining dynamism with purpose.

As all the original manuscripts were written on papyrus (of vegetable origin) or parchment (dried animal skins), we are reliant on a long succession of copyists for the texts we have today. So how can we be sure, knowing the errors of omission and addition inherent in any copying process over such vast spans of time, that we have reliable texts? Surprisingly, copies exist of parts of the Greek NT which predate the first authoritative collections of the Hebrew and Aramaic scriptures. In fact, such was the impetus in the early churches to obtain copies of the Epistles and Gospels that the number of extant copies of all or part of the NT made before around 600 AD runs to about 5,000. This far exceeds the numbers of extant manuscripts of any other ancient text – even Caesar's Gallic War has come down to us in only ten good copies, the oldest being from the late 10th century.[9] Because there are so many copies, the science of textual criticism has, down the ages, made it possible to detect and correct the minor textual corruptions to which the most careful copyists were (and are) prey.

When the English Revised Version was produced in 1884, the earliest manuscript of the entire OT available to the translators was the standard Jewish 'Masoretic' text[10] in a copy dated 916AD. The reason for this late date lies in the extreme veneration of copies of the Jewish scriptures by the rabbis – worn-out copies were not retained and punctilious care was taken to avoid copying errors as far as humanly possible. Comparison with earlier copies discovered during the last century testifies to the accuracy of the copying process directed by generations of Jewish scholars to preserve the original scriptures in Hebrew, which had long ceased to be the everyday language of the Jewish people. God is His own witness as to its reliability – *"I am watching to see that my word is fulfilled."*[11]

The Canon of the Bible

When the risen Lord instructed his disciples during the forty days between His resurrection and ascension, He was careful to set God's eternal purpose in a context which would be meaningful to them. *"Everything must be fulfilled"*, He said, *"that is written about me in the Law of Moses, the Prophets and the Psalms."*[12] This clear statement surely satisfies His disciples in every age that these three types of OT writing – together comprising much of that Testament – are to be regarded as 'canonical',[13] reckoned as Holy Scripture. Further, this statement underlines the essential continuity between the two Testaments – they are both about Him!

But what about the remaining parts of the OT? Although it is rarely safe to argue from a negative, the Lord, who was so incisive in identifying and censuring unscriptural Jewish traditions and practices, never questioned (and often referred to) the writings which had long been accepted as holy scripture by the Jewish nation. There were, of course, other writings – the Apocrypha - which by His time had not received this endorsement. These writings are of four types – historical, wisdom and ethical, apocalyptic, and religious fiction. While interesting, they were not accepted as authoritative by the Jewish religious establishment or, unlike the canonical OT, referred to by the Lord. The collective wisdom of Protestant Christianity has followed the Jewish tradition.

Turning to the NT, we are not presented with any strong rival claims to canonicity. The very few Gnostic texts which today attract a disproportionate amount of publicity[14] and purported gospels and epistles are datable to the 2nd to 4th centuries AD, and are clearly at odds with the NT record. The widespread and rapid acceptance of the NT scriptures in 'the early church' was attributable simply to their authority. The Epistles were widely copied, collected and circulated from the earliest times because Christians knew who wrote them and were convinced of their authority as men who had known (or seen) the Lord. The Gospels followed, because their authors made it their business to write authoritatively about *"all that Jesus began to do and to teach".*[15] Nobody imposed a canon of NT scriptures on 'the early church' – the two grew up organically together, no doubt under the guidance of Him who *"will guide you into all truth."*[16]

The Consolidation of the Bible

Since 1948, Biblical scholarship has been immensely assisted by the discovery of the Dead Sea Scrolls, enabling about 100 books of the Old Testament to be partially reconstructed from fragments[17] dating back as far as the first century BC. Comparison of these ancient documents with the much later authoritative 'Masoretic' text shows remarkably few differences and, in some instances, has helped elucidate the meaning of difficult texts in the later version. The textual study of the huge number of fragments continues, and further elucidation will no doubt result. As for the NT, it is now possible for scholars to cross-check the text with evidence as old as the mid second century – again, there are few divergencies from later copies.

Finally, one further key factor linking both Testaments is the famous Septuagint – a Greek translation of the OT and Apocrypha made around 200 BC. As well as throwing light upon the precise meaning of abstruse Hebrew expressions,[18] the Septuagint provided the classical world with an accessible version of the Jewish scriptures, just at the time when it was required by the exploding Christian mission. It is hard not to discern the providence of God not merely in the inspiration of Scripture but also in its dissemination.

[1] Ps.19:1-2; [2] Rom.1:19-20; [3] John 1:1; [4] John 5:39; [5] John 14:26; [6] Gal.1:11-20; [7] 2 Tim.3:16-17; [8] 2 Pet.1:21; [9] See chap. 14 of F.F. Bruce: The Books and the Parchments, revised edition 1991, which includes a telling summary of the reliability of NT attestation and an explanation of how textual criticism works; [10] Derived from the Hebrew word for 'tradition'; [11] Jer.1:12; [12] Luke 24:44; [13] From the Greek word *kanon*, signifying a measuring rod or standard [14] And the attentions of novelists like Dan Brown; [15] Acts 1:1; [16] John 16:13. When the Synod of Hippo in AD393 listed the NT canon, it was merely recording what had long been accepted as authoritative throughout most of Christendom; [17] There is one complete book - a parchment scroll of Isaiah – which survived in the particular microclimate of the Qumran caves; [18] One well-known example is the cognate Greek words which the Septuagint translators used to render expressions connected to the Hebrew word *kipper* (atonement), which extend our understanding of the meaning of these words and their connections in Hebrew.

Bible quotations from the NIV.

CHAPTER TEN: READING THE BIBLE FOR ALL ITS WORTH (KARL SMITH)

The watchman sat, under the light at the front of the church hall, poring over his Bible. The sounds of night on the edge of an African city could be heard: the barking of dogs, the hum of crickets, and the occasional cry of a baby awakening in a neighbouring house. He had been learning to read at the church's adult literacy classes and at last he could read the Bible for himself. Whilst we may take our ability to read for granted, we must never take for granted the privilege of being able to read God's own message in God's own words to us whenever we like.

Daily Reading

We should all make time to read at least something from the Bible each day. Most find that first thing in the morning is the best time to do this. I'm not at all a morning person, but I have discovered that if you listen to God before the Devil has a chance to speak to you through the many means at his disposal, you'll be better equipped to face the day with the right attitude. It is easier to begin the day with God than to try to reclaim the day for Him later on. Time spent with the Scriptures in the morning is a briefing from our commanding officer and is essential to find out what He wants us to do for the day. Ezekiel found that, '*In the morning, the word of the LORD came to me*'.[1] Isaiah, speaking for the Messiah, said, '*Morning by morning he awakens; he awakens my ear to hear as those who are taught*'.[2]

Sure enough, when we get to the Gospels, we find the Lord Jesus rising very early in the morning to spend time with His Father.[3] Some call this their quiet time, but the name isn't important. Whatever you call it, identify a consistent place for it your daily routine and a place where you won't be interrupted. It is easier to begin the day with God than to try to reclaim the day for Him later on.

Top tips: The following are some ideas people have shared with me about how to structure a quiet time. Different ones will help different people:

1. Briefly ask God to help you understand the passage.
2. Don't try to read too much at a sitting.
3. Follow something systematically, such as a book of the Bible.
4. Vary the Old and New Testament in your reading. A reading plan that takes you through the whole Bible in one or more years can be helpful.
5. It might help to read a short passage slowly and more than once so that it sinks in. I personally find this of more value than reading pages and pages.
6. Repeat the words to God, especially ones about Himself, His Son and His Spirit.
7. Look for something about the character of the Lord Jesus to treasure through the day.
8. Look for a command to obey or an example to follow. It may be a negative example to avoid. Above all ask God to help you obey it.
9. Some keep a diary noting in two or three sentences what was in the passage they read.
10. If a phrase or a verse has struck you, memorise it and repeat it to yourself throughout the day.

Bible Study

Your Bible reading does not work like a 'horoscope'. Each chapter you are reading is a part of the story of God's dealings with mankind. That's why a separate time of Bible study is important to get a sense of how each section relates to the whole.

At least once in your life, you should read the Bible right through from cover to cover. Read another chapter or two in your armchair instead of watching some rubbish on the television that you're not even interested in anyway, on a train or bus journey, while you're having a lie-in, just as you would read any other book. Start at Genesis and go through to Revelation. Only then can you be confident that you've read it all with a sense of the whole narrative.

More regularly, however, we need to sit down and look at the themes of the Bible. We can study a person's life, looking at the various passages that speak about him or her. We can study a place in the Bible, building up a picture of what happened there. We may want to work out what the Bible says about a particular issue we have encountered in our disciple life. On the other hand, we may wish to understand why the church does something a particular way. We may wish to follow through a theme that has fascinated us, like the feelings experienced by the Lord Jesus, prayers of godly people or the House of God throughout history.

One tool that is very useful in anything like this is the cross-referencing system in many Bibles. The little letters next to phrases in some editions of the Bible refer you to other verses where the same word or phrase is used or which deal with a similar theme. Be aware that these are only the verses that have occurred to particular editors and may reflect their denominational background. There may be many other verses you can consider on the same theme. They're not inspired like the Bible itself but are put there by human beings to help us navigate our way round the Bible.

Another tool you can use is a concordance or list of words used in the Bible. This is a valuable way of finding all the places in scripture that deal with a certain topic. You can also use a concordance to see how a word that has been puzzling us in one verse is used throughout the rest of the Bible. Very often this leads to a much clearer understanding of what it means.

The Bible is a translation of Greek and Hebrew documents, no matter what language we read it in. Some concordances allow you to see which Greek or Hebrew word is being translated by every English word. This can be extremely useful for seeing that a particular word in our English Bible is normally translated from a different word in the Greek or Hebrew. You can then see where that Greek or Hebrew word is used elsewhere in the Bible in a book called a lexicon. Doing this links scriptures that we might not otherwise connect in our minds. Even for those of us not fluent in these ancient languages, we can still get a feel for the original text.

Other books can fill in the picture of what life was like at the time and see the Bible in context. Bible study has never been more accessible than in the current computer age. A number of programmes allow you to use a concordance in several different versions of the Bible at once, a click shows you which Greek or Hebrew word has been used and another click take you to the lexicon. All of these can be kept open on the screen in front of you – much easier than keeping your finger in several pages of a book at once! Another click points you to relevant commentaries. It's God's Word just the same whether it appears on the screen or the printed page. Nevertheless, whilst concordances, commentaries and lexicons are useful, we must repeat again that it is the Bible itself that is inspired. The rest are simply aids to help us understand it.

What Can We Expect to Find in the Bible?

"... you have been acquainted with the sacred writings, which are able to make you wise for salvation through faith in Christ Jesus. All scripture is breathed out by God and profitable for teaching, for reproof, for correction, and for training in righteousness, that the man of God may be competent, equipped for every good work.[4]

Firstly, the Bible teaches us how to be saved. Then, by the various processes described here, it equips us for every good work. For the Christian, the point of reading the Bible is to help us to do good to others in this world and to glorify God. Worthwhile Bible study will eventually lead to a clearer understanding of God's will and give us something to obey practically. He won't reveal more until we've obeyed what he's already given us. We will never exhaust the riches of the Bible or get tired of learning its message to us.

[1] Ez.12.8; [2] Is.50:4; [3] Mark 1:35; [4] 2 Tim.3:15-17

Bible quotations from the ESV.

CHAPTER ELEVEN: THE LORD'S RETURN (CRAIG JONES)

In 1995, a series of sixteen fictional novels began to be published, which, over the following twelve years, would amass total sales in excess of 65 million copies. Seven of the series have held the top slot on the *New York Times* Best Sellers list between 2000 and 2005. The 'Left Behind' series, by Tim LaHaye and Jerry B. Jenkins, has certainly propelled the subject of biblical end-times prophecies into the imaginations of mainstream literary fiction consumers over recent years.

Whilst clearly fictional in nature, these novels are nevertheless claimed to be based on teachings contained in the Bible. However, there is no full agreement amongst the various Christian denominations as to the 'true' interpretation of these biblical teachings. Whilst it is possible to establish certain future events as biblical 'fact', the precise detail and timing can be the subject of much speculation. Arguably, perhaps, the most astonishing event that will trigger the unfolding of a whole series of major prophetic events, will be the return of the Lord Jesus Christ.

The Lord Himself declared, *"... I will come again and receive you to Myself ..."* clearly stating His intention to return for His disciples after going to be with His Father in heaven following His death and resurrection.[1] In confirmation of this, the angel who appeared to the awestruck disciples on the Mount of Olives, immediately after they had witnessed the Lord ascend to heaven in the clouds, said, *"This Jesus, who has been taken up from you into heaven, will come in just the same way as you have watched Him go into heaven."*[2] The apostle Paul also confirms this truth in 1 Thessalonians 4:13-18, from which we glean the expression 'the rapture' (not a word found in the English translations of the Bible, but meaning 'taken up into heaven' from Latin *'raptus'* – taken away).

Associated at some point with our Lord's return is something the Lord Himself describes as 'a great tribulation'.[3] It's a time of unparalleled worldwide suffering, and oppression at the hands of someone identified in 2 Thessalonians 2:3 as *the man of lawlessness*, who rises to such a position of global prominence and influence that he eventually sets himself up as being 'god', exalting himself above the one true God in a rebuilt 'temple of God' in Jerusalem.[4] This fits with the Lord's description of the 'abomination of desolation' in Matthew 24:15. The global acceptance of the authority of this 'man of lawlessness' will be sealed by the significance of the covenant that he will make with Israel at the start of the 70th week of Daniel's prophecy.[5] According to Daniel 9:27, the abomination of desolation will occur halfway through this 7-year covenant period.

When all this is linked to *"the coming of our Lord Jesus Christ and our gathering together to Him"*,[6] a view emerges that the Lord's coming to the air for His Church does not take place until the man of lawlessness exalts himself in this way, at that time. Hence, in this 'mid-tribulation' view,[7] the rapture can be precisely dated from the moment the covenant is struck, which is quite likely to be a widely publicised event at the time, thereby allowing a calculation to be made, arriving at 3½ years after the signing of the covenant, immediately before the great tribulation proper. However, this is inconsistent with the clear weight of scriptural evidence regarding the coming of the Lord as being both imminent and unknown.[8]

Another similar ('post-tribulation') view exists based in part on the same argument (and therefore subject to the same weakness), which further delays the rapture of Church-age believers in the Lord Jesus to be coincident with His return to the earth to judge the nations[2] and to establish His 1000-year reign of peace.[10] The implication of this is, of course, that believers in the Lord Jesus will have to live through the great tribulation. This view at first may seem supported by verses such as John 16:33 and 17:15 with regard to the 'requirement' for tribulation suffering. However, this requires a rather narrow definition of 'tribulation' as referring specifically to this prophetic period. And yet a survey of the occurrences of this word in the New Testament reveals a very general usage that includes any collective or personal circumstances of trials of faith.[11]

An historical justification is also cited in support of this viewpoint, as, it is argued, this was evidently the belief of the early church fathers and is reflected in their writings and therefore the absence of teaching by them on any alternative understanding demonstrates a 'taken-for-granted' acceptance of the view. Anything 'new' and divergent is therefore presumed not to be tenable. We might wonder what would have happened if that kind of stance had prevailed in the times of the Reformation, when the great doctrine of justification by faith was considered 'novel' and therefore dangerous, according to the received wisdom and understanding of the time.

So what are we to make of all this? It's significant to note that when Paul writes about this subject[12] it is intended to bring comfort and encouragement to the believers, and therefore to us also. Surely, it's difficult to find comfort in the prospect of having to endure the horrors of a time of tribulation that the Lord says will be *"... such as has not occurred since the beginning of the world until now, nor ever will."*[13] The comfort is in the knowledge that all those who have accepted the Lord Jesus Christ as their Saviour, from the time of His death and resurrection to the moment when He will appear in the clouds, will be graciously and miraculously transported from the earth to enjoy the presence of the Lord and take up their promised residence in His Father's house.[14]

We find further support for this in 1 Thessalonians 1:10 and 5:9, which promise deliverance from the wrath of God which will be meted out in righteous judgement in these end times. The return of the Lord Jesus is therefore best viewed as presented to us as being accomplished in two phases. The first is when He comes to the air to take all believers of this present Church age to their heavenly inheritance.[15] The second phase then takes place at the end of the tribulation period, when, in accordance with the prophecy in Zechariah 14:4, the Lord will actually stand again as Son of Man upon the earth, on the Mount of Olives, to begin His deliverance of Israel from their oppressors and also to judge the nations of the earth and usher in His glorious 1000-year reign of global peace and prosperity, as the great Prince of Peace.

What is the Tribulation?

- It's uniquely 'great' – as opposed to various trials experienced by Christians (Matt. 24:21-28; Rev.7:14)
- It's primarily and specifically the 'time of Jacob's trouble' (Jer.30:7-8 NKJV)
- The 'elect' are therefore believing Jews during the Tribulation; as distinct from Christ's Church (Matt.24:22)
- Its purpose is to purge Israel and destroy Gentile world power
- Thus Matt.24:31,41 are not describing the rapture of the Church, but a different, subsequent gathering

[1] John 14:2-3; [2] Acts 1:11; [3] Matt.24:9-28; [4] see 2 Thess.2:3-10; [5] Dan.9:24-27, where the 'weeks' are understood to represent periods of 7 years as found in Revelation; [6] 2 Thess.2:1-4; [7] some refer this

term tribulation to the whole 70th week; but in this article it is the 2nd half thereof; [8] e.g. Phil.3:20; 1 Cor.15:51-52; Acts 1:7; 1 Thess.5:1-2; [9] Matt.25:31-32; [10] Rev.20:1-4; [11] e.g. Matt.13:21; Acts 7:10; 11:19; Rom.12:12; 1 Thess.1:6; [12] 1 Thess.4:18; 5:11 particularly; [13] Matt.24:21; [14] John 14:1-3; [15] 1 Thess.4:15-18

Bible quotations are from the NASB.

CHAPTER TWELVE: HE'S COMING SOON (DAVID WOODS)

It's inevitable. At what has become known as 'The Rapture', our Saviour will come to take all born-again believers to be with Him forever. It will be an 'out of this world' gathering in the clouds where those who have died secure 'in Christ' will be raised first, and we who are alive, also secure 'in Christ', will be caught up to meet them. And so will begin the reality of our wonderful eternal existence with our Lord.[1] That day will be all about the fulfilment of Christ's promise to return for His Church, the Body of Christ, and is referred to as the 'Day of Christ'[2] which is different from 'the Day of the Lord'[3] and 'the Day of God'[4] that denote periods to follow after.

"If I go and prepare a place for you, I will come again and receive you to Myself, that where I am, there you may be also,"[5] were words the early disciples wouldn't forget. They lived each day with the Lord's promise ringing in their ears, excitedly anticipating His return. When He didn't return within their expected timescales some started to doubt, and outsiders started to mock saying, *"Where is the promise of His coming?"*[6] Given that 2,000 years or so have passed since then, we might be guilty of the same, but we must be aware that Christ did not say when He would return. He is waiting for that moment when, according to God's eternal purposes, He will come to receive His Church.[7] It's not for us to try to second-guess God's timing, because it's entirely different from ours![8] We must live expecting Him at any time!

William Barclay helpfully tells us that the Greek word *parousia*, usually translated 'coming' in verses which refer to Christ's return,[9] was used in other Greek documents contemporary with the New Testament to denote the arrival or the actual presence of a dignitary, usually the Roman emperor. 'One of the commonest things is that provinces dated a new era from the *parousia* of the emperor ... a new section of time emerged with the coming ... another common practice was to strike new coins to commemorate the visitation ... it was as if ... a new set of values had emerged.'[10] The *parousia* of One so much greater than any earthly ruler is imminent. It is sensible that we prepare ourselves, and look forward to that new era where God's high values and standards will be maintained forever.

I remember how a realisation of the Lord's return, and the prospect of my being 'left behind', made me come to the Saviour to know for certain that I would be one of those to meet Him in the air. If you don't have that assurance, look to Calvary and realise the lengths that God and His Son went to in order to secure your salvation from the consequences of your sin. Request and accept the forgiveness for sin that God offers through the sacrifice of Christ. You'll then be ready to be called to that gathering in the air, and to eternity beyond. Be sure to be ready.

As Christians, a fresh realisation of the 'anytime soon' return of our Lord should also fuel our desire to ensure that those we work with, study with, socialise with, engage with, are made aware of the *'living hope'* that is ours.[11] Demonstrating by our actions that our lives are governed by heavenly standards so very different from those of this world and seizing opportunities to speak of *"Christ ... the hope of glory"*[12] will witness to the fact that *"our citizenship is in heaven"*,[13] and that we *"wait for His Son from heaven."*[14] **Living in the light of the Lord's imminent return should galvanise our efforts to lead others to Christ.**

Those *"who are Christ's at His coming"*[15] should be ready. The reality of the Lord's return can often be overshadowed by the mundane matters of life, or by the busyness of the legitimate things of Christian service. There is a daily need to focus our attention on our Saviour and His promise, *"... behold, I am coming quickly ... Yes, I am coming quickly."*[16]

Service for our Master will be reviewed at the 'judgment seat of Christ'.[17] We must be ready to give account![18] John wrote, *"abide in Him, so that when He appears, we may have confidence and not shrink away from Him in shame at His coming".*[19] What occupies our time these days? Are we fully absorbed in our jobs, our families and our possessions? Are we continually distracted by entertainments, such as the Internet world at our fingertips? Are we giving any quality time to God in service? Are we 'abiding in Him'?

The Scriptures teach us that it's not the quantity of service that Christ will review, but the quality. Our aim should be to give of our best, offering service of the highest quality, according to God's standards, as guided and directed by Him. Take a look at 1 Corinthians 3:10-15. Often misinterpreted, this scripture should be properly understood in its context: the work of quality building within the House of God. It's here, in churches of God that together form God's house today, where men and women should render service that is precious in the sight of God. **Living in the light of the Lord's imminent return should make us want to surrender our lives and do the best we can in obedience to God's will.**

John also wrote, *when He appears, we will be like Him.*[20] That's glorious! Our earthly bodies exchanged for something far superior, just like His, made ready for eternal glory! John reminds us that, by being absorbed by the certain hope of Christ's return, personal purity should be the result: *"Everyone who has this hope fixed on Him purifies himself, just as He is pure*".[21] Christ's return will usher in a new era of purity and holiness, but God commands His people to be holy today.[22] We struggle with sin, but we thank God for the provision of 1 John 1:9, whereby forgiveness and cleansing can be sought through confession of daily sin that spoils our walk. **Living in the light of the Lord's imminent return should have the effect of purifying our lives.**

James told his readers to *"be patient ... until the coming of the Lord ... strengthen your hearts, for the coming of the Lord is near"*.[23] It's not easy living in a world that is so opposed to God's ways, enduring incessant attacks that attempt to undermine our faith. We must learn patience, despite our desire to be removed and to be with the Lord.[24] In the knowledge that being with the Lord will be *"very much better"*[25] our hearts, our emotions and our love should be strengthened in the face of the enemy's attempts to keep us earthbound. **Living in the light of the Lord's imminent return should strengthen our hearts despite discouragement and trial.**

Having such a certain future is what makes the New Testament word 'hope' so wonderful. We have a certainty of a future, secured and promised by God, brought to us through Christ and sealed by the indwelling Holy Spirit. Today, the people of God also lay hold of a hope that is a present-day reality.[26] We're to grip it tight, lay hold of it, realising that it brings us presently before God, in spirit, to experience the delights of His presence in advance of the day we're waiting expectantly for! This is the joy of the worship of the people of God, invited into His presence to appreciate something of His eternal glory and grace. This hope is anchored *'within the veil'* of the heavenly tabernacle, not made with hands,[27] and linked with Jesus having entered there *"as a forerunner for us, having become a high priest forever"*.[28] He's in the glory, and as a result we have the privilege to join

Him in spiritual worship each week, and have a little taster of what the future holds as we *"enter the holy place by the blood of Jesus"*.[29] **Living in the light of the imminence of the Lord's return should enhance our worship and appreciation of Christ our Saviour.**

The wonderful future that is being prepared for us should make us cry out, *"Maranatha"*,[30] "O Lord, come!" Until then, let's live in the light of His imminent return!

[1] 1 Thess.4:6-11; [2] Phil.1:6,10; 2:16; [3] many OT refs and 2 Pet.3:10; [4] 2 Pet.3:12; [5] John 14:3; [6] 2 Pet.3:4; [7] Eph.5:27; [8] see 2 Pet.3:8; [9] e.g. 1 Thess.2:19; 4:15; Jas.5:7,8; 1 John 2:28; [10] William Barclay, New Testament Words; [11] 1 Pet.1:3; [12] Col.1:27; [13] Phil.3:20; [14] 1 Thess.1:10; [15] 1 Cor.15:23; [16] Rev.22:7,20; [17] 2 Cor.5:10; [18] Rom.14:12; [19] 1 John 2:28; [20] 1 John 3:2; [21] 1 John 3:3; [22] 1 Pet.1:16; [23] Jas.5:7-8; [24] see 2 Cor.5:2; [25] Phil.1:23; [26] Heb.6:18; [27] Heb.9:11; [28] Heb.6:20; [29] Heb.10:19-23; [30] 1 Cor.16:22

Bible quotations from the NASB.

CHAPTER THIRTEEN: SPIRITUAL GIFTS (ALEX REID)

Who is the Giver of Gifts?

The answer is the Triune God. Father, Son and Spirit are all presented in Scripture as the source of spiritual gifts. In Romans 12:3,6 God the Father is the one allotting to each a measure of faith, producing gift according to the proportion of faith. Ephesians 4:7–12 clearly identifies the Lord Jesus as the giver of the gifted types of people listed. While 1 Corinthians 12:11 tells us that the gifts are distributed by the Holy Spirit according to His will.

Who are the Recipients of the Gifts?

In 1 Corinthians 12:7,11,18 the expression 'each one' is addressed to the Corinthians in the overall context of their membership of the Church the Body of Christ. Ephesians 4:7-16 also uses the term 'each one'[1] in the same Body of Christ context. The conclusion therefore must be that the recipients of the gifts are all individual members of the Church the Body. It is entirely possible that individual Body members can be endowed with more than one gift. What gift and how many a believer might be given is according to the sovereign will of the Holy Spirit.[2]

What is the Nature of the Gifts?

In the original Scriptures the Greek word used of a spiritual gift is the singular noun *charisma* which is derived from the word *charis*, meaning grace. W.E. Vine says of charisma: 'a gift involving grace (*charis*) on the part of God as the Donor.'[3] This singular noun is used of the gift of eternal life[4] and of a spiritual gift.[5] The plural of *charisma* is *charismata*, which is used of the spiritual gifts bestowed on believers.[6] The important point is that all God's gifts are as a result of His grace. Therefore spiritual gifts are the visible effects of the grace of God; the concrete expressions of that grace.

It is interesting to note that the word used for gift in Ephesians 4:8 is *doma*, which Vine says, 'lends greater stress to the concrete character of the gift, than to its beneficent nature.'[7]

What is the Purpose of the Gifts?

Hebrews 2:3-4 gives a principal purpose of the gifts, that is, the authentication of the witness of the apostles. Another purpose is the nurturing and well-being of the Church the Body of Christ. 1 Corinthians 12:7 tells us that the manifestations of the Spirit are *'for the common good'*, the common good being the building up of the saints in their common membership of Christ's Body. Ephesians 4:11-12 leaves us in no doubt that the gifts listed were for *"the equipping of the saints for the work of service, to the building up of the body of Christ."*

How Can I Tell What My Gift Might Be?

In identifying our individual gifts the following comment from J.I. Packer is helpful: 'When, therefore, Christians are said to "have gifts" (Rom.12:6), the meaning is not that they are outstandingly brilliant or efficient (they may be, they may not; it varies), but rather that God has observably used them to edification in specific ways already, and this warrants the expectation that he will do the same again.'[8] In other words, it is in our effective service that our gift or gifts will come to light.

How Can I Distinguish a Spiritual Gift from a Natural Ability?

The remainder of the above quote from Packer gives an answer to this question: 'We need to draw a clear distinction between man's capacity to perform and God's prerogative to bless, for it is God's use of our abilities rather than the abilities themselves that constitute charismata. If no regular, identifiable spiritual benefit for others or ourselves results from what we do, we should not think of our capacity to do it as a spiritual gift.'[2]

Do All the Spiritual Gifts Still Operate Today?

The following classification of the spiritual gifts gives a good starting point from which to answer this question:

1. Those necessarily involving miraculous expression – apostleship, gifts of healings, workings of miracles, diverse kinds of tongues, interpretation of tongues.
2. Those which may or may not require miraculous expression – prophecy, the word of wisdom and the word of knowledge, faith, discerning of spirits.
3. Those which do not in any case require miraculous expression – e.g. teachers, helps, governments, ministry, pastors.[10] (Of course, we are not denying divine enablement as distinct from miraculous expression.)

The gifts in categories 2 and 3 above are still in operation today, although those in category 2 need some qualification (see 'The Holy Spirit and the Believer' cited above). Those in group 1, which we will call sign gifts, are no longer in operation, since their purpose has been fulfilled. They belong to the apostolic era, their stated purpose being to authenticate the witness of the Apostles and those immediately associated with them.[11]

This is in accord with the pattern established throughout Scripture. Each new 'dispensation' (i.e. phase of God's working) opens with a cluster of miracles which mark its beginning. The dispensation of the Law began with the miracles associated with Moses and Joshua. The age of the prophets opens with the miracles worked by Elijah and Elisha; and that of the New Testament era by those of the Lord and his apostles. Each cluster of miracles lasts approximately two generations; each dispensation closing with a distinct lack of miraculous signs.

It is acknowledged that not all Christians would concur with the view just given, but would claim that the miraculous gifts are still available to men and women of faith today. This view usually rests on particular interpretations of certain scriptures and an appeal to the visible effects of so-called miraculous gifts. Space precludes an exhaustive examination of them all, but we will look at one scriptural interpretation and one claimed miraculous effect.

The following quotation is offered as an example of an argument used to support the continuation of the sign gifts: '... strong evidence for the permanence of charismata ... is found in 1 Corinthians 13:8-12, where Paul envisages them as continuing to be manifest until the *parousia*.'[12] The proposition being advanced is that all the gifts will continue until the second coming of Christ.

Verse 12 of 1 Corinthians 13 does seem to envisage a future time when the believer will be face to face with Christ, but is this the same experience as the coming perfection mentioned in verse 10? In verses 8 and 9, the permanence of love is being contrasted with the temporary nature of the gifts of prophecy, tongues and miraculous knowledge. These gifts would cease when a stage of perfection in the sense of maturity or completeness was reached.[13] When the full revelation of God's Word was completed in terms of *"the faith which was once for all handed down to the saints"*,[14] the temporary and partial expedients of prophecy, tongues and miraculous knowledge no longer had a purpose.

To emphasise this, the apostle uses the illustration of his own growth from childhood to adult maturity. The speech, thinking and reasoning of childhood which were put away when reaching maturity are equivalent to the partial gifts of tongues, prophecy and knowledge. This allusion to growth from childhood to adult maturity was particularly relevant to the church in Corinth, which was displaying lack of spiritual maturity in that it was a church divided by faction while placing an undue emphasis on the exercise of miraculous gifts.

Having made his point about partial compared to full revelation in verses 8-11, Paul in verse 12 now applies the same principle in another secondary way. He sees even our understanding of the full revelation of Scripture as being partial in comparison with the completeness of our understanding when we shall see Christ face to face.

Those who claim to exercise miraculous gifts today point to the supposed effectiveness of healing campaigns as an evidence of the continuation of the sign gifts. However, these campaigns differ notably from the pattern provided first by the Lord Himself and then the apostles. Their healing was always successful, instant, complete, lasting and included even restoration of crippled or incomplete limbs. Moreover, it is often found that those who claim miraculous spiritual gifts today are found in error in key issues in their doctrine (e.g. eternal salvation), so caution is appropriate and the teaching of 'miracle workers' should be brought to the test of Scripture. The following quote from J.I. Packer gives a succinct and clear analysis of the proposition: 'Can charismatic healing ministries be convincingly equated with the healing gifts mentioned in 1 Corinthians 12: 28, 30? Surely not.'

[1] Eph.4:7; [2] 1 Cor.12:11; [3] W.E. Vine, Expository Dictionary of New Testament Words; [4] Rom.6:23; [5] 1 Pet.4:10; [6] Rom.12:6; 1 Cor.12:4; [7] W.E. Vine, Expository Dictionary of New Testament Words; [8] J.I. Packer, *Keep In Step With The Spirit*, p.84; [9] *Ibid.*; [10] G. Prasher, *The Holy Spirit and The Believer.* Hayes Press; [11] Heb.2:3-4; [12] New Bible Dictionary, Inter Varsity Press, 1996 edition, p.1130; [13] 1 Cor.13:10; [14] Jude 3

Bible quotations are from the NASB.

CHAPTER FOURTEEN: USING OUR GIFTS TO GOD'S GLORY (STEPHEN HICKLING)

Have you ever bought a gift for someone (a box of chocolates, perhaps) and then been asked to share in it by the recipient of the gift? Many of us will be used to spending a lot of time selecting gifts worth giving. How nice it can be when the person receiving the gift deems it to be worth sharing! The value of the shared-out gift must have made such an impression on the young boy of John 6. Five small barley loaves and two fish were given, received by the Lord and shared out. The result: five thousand men (let alone women and children) fed and twelve baskets of leftovers gathered up!

When we are first saved we enjoy God's gifts for ourselves: we're excited to receive the free gift of God, which is eternal life in Christ Jesus our Lord;[1] and we're amazed that God adds to that every spiritual blessing in the heavenly places in Christ.[2] But as we mature in Christian life, we start to realise that God desires that we share what He has given us for His glory. So it is with the spiritual gifts which we have received.

Discovering Our Gifts

These spiritual gifts are not reserved for an elite group. Scripture clearly establishes the fact that every member of the body of Christ, that is every believer, has received at least one gift; there are no useless members in the church which is His body.[3] Spiritual gifts are not to be confused with our natural abilities and talents. Whilst the latter may be used in our service for the Lord, the spiritual gifts must be exercised in that sphere. For those seeking to identify their own gift or gifts, the following practical tips may be of assistance:

- Familiarise yourself with the range of gifts available and take time to understand how they are seen in practice. The three key passages of scripture are: Romans 12:6-13; 1 Corinthians 12:8-28; and Ephesians 4:11.
- Pray that God will make your gift(s) clear to you as you read His Word and engage in service. Consider also how the Spirit leads you to make intercession in prayer for the needs of others and take note of answered prayers.
- Read and study the Word of God regularly. Daily reading prepares us to meet the needs of others. Think about how you commonly apply your Bible reading; that will be a strong indication of your gift.
- Look for fruit and fulfilment in service. God-given peace coupled with evident fruitfulness will be present where spiritual gifts are being properly exercised.
- Take advice from others. Your overseers, in particular, should be willing to talk to you about your gift(s) and the ways in which it (or they) might be best used within your local church.
- Keep your motives for service in check. If love is not the driving force behind everything we do for the Lord, our service will be in vain.[4]

The gifts of the Spirit reveal the bountifulness of our God and the endless supply of His grace.

Developing our Gifts

So far as exercising our gifts is concerned, God's Word tells us that we are to "be *good stewards of the manifold grace of God*".[5] Quite simply, God's grace comes to us in many different shapes and sizes, but it's always sufficient: meeting every need at every time. The gifts of the

Spirit reveal the bountifulness of our God and the endless supply of His grace. The gifts have been given to us as 'stewards' or 'managers', that is as servants in charge of the house and possessions of the Master. Our job is not simply to sit on what we have or to keep it for our own enjoyment. The steward is to administer or distribute: not carelessly, but at the proper time and as required to meet each need. Will the Lord find us operating as good stewards of our gifts when He returns?[6]

With this in mind, Peter encourages us to hold nothing back, exercising our gifts to the fullest extent of our God-given ability. To do so will require that you *"do not neglect your gift"*,[7] but rather keep it in regular use by serving others in the area for which God has gifted you.

[1] Rom.6:23; [2] Eph.1:3; [3] Rom.12:3; 1 Cor.12:7; Eph.4:7; 1 Pet.4:10; [4] 1 Cor. 13:1-3; [5] 1 Pet.4:10 NASB; [6] Luke 12:42-43; [7] 1 Tim. 4:14 NIV

CHAPTER FIFTEEN: THE CHURCH AND CHURCHES OF GOD (JAMES NEEDHAM)

"On this rock I will build My church, and the gates of Hades shall not prevail against it."[1] This triumphant declaration, made with the shadow of Calvary looming ever closer,[2] has thrilled disciples of the Lord Jesus Christ ever since He began that majestic spiritual work, anticipated at Caesarea Philippi, of building His Church, a body undefiled, incorruptible and unassailable by all the powers of the Enemy.

The Church, His Body: 'The Mystery of Christ'

In describing the pre-eminence of the risen, exalted Christ, the Apostle Paul refers to His position as *'head over all things'* and also refers to *'the church, which is His body, the fullness of Him who fills all in all'*.[3] That believing Gentiles should be brought together with believing Jews to be fellow heirs, members of the same body, is called *'the mystery of Christ'*,[4] hidden through the ages in God, yet now *'revealed by the Spirit to His holy apostles and prophets.*[5]

Throughout his epistles, Paul reveals more concerning this Church. It is composed of believers on the Lord Jesus Christ,[6] who have been cleansed by the Word[7] and baptised in the Holy Spirit.[8] It is now the means by which *"the manifold wisdom of God might be made known ... to the principalities and powers in the heavenly places".*[9] It is precious to Him[10] and in a coming day He will present that Church to Himself as a bride *"not having spot or wrinkle or any such thing"*,[11] all glorious in bright garments!

This great building project began at Pentecost, when those gathered in Jerusalem were baptised in the Holy Spirit according to the promise of the Father.[12] There the Lord Jesus began to build, binding together those who believed in His name into an unseen body, *'the fullness of Him'* to whom all fullness belongs.[13] It is an enterprise which continues today through the work of the gospel, and will not be complete until He comes to claim His own, when both living believers and *'the dead in Christ'* will be united to meet the Lord in the air.[14]

The Church and the Churches of God

The Greek word translated 'church' in our Bibles literally means 'a called-out gathering'. The Church, His Body is a gathering of those who have responded to the call of the gospel,[15] but an examination of the New Testament use of the word 'church' reveals that not all references refer to this company. When Stephen stood before the Sanhedrin, he recounted Israel's early history as *'the congregation* [literally 'church'] *in the wilderness'*,[16] having been called out of Egypt by the command of God through Moses that they might serve Him. Yet Israel's passage through the wilderness cannot be associated with the progress of the Church, His Body, since the Lord made clear in Matthew 16 that the building of this Church was a future project.

Similarly, in Acts 19 we read of Demetrius' call to the men of Ephesus to join together against the preaching of Paul. Although many answered his call, *"the assembly* [literally 'church'] *was confused"*, and the city clerk recommended that proper enquiry be made to the city authority, *"the lawful assembly"* ('church').[17] Though described by the same Greek word, the rabble assembled by Demetrius to contend against the gospel had no connection whatsoever with the spotless gathering constructed by Christ on the basis of gospel acceptance.

So we are compelled to conclude that not every use of the word 'church' in the New Testament pertains to the same gathering. What then of the 'church of God', often referred to in the New Testament? Since the inception of NT magazine, it has been consistently taught that the Scriptures draw a crucial distinction between 'the Church, His Body' and 'the churches of God'. Nor is this distinction an academic matter. It is our conviction that an understanding of the divine will for disciples today still requires this vital distinction to be observed, that we may rightly divide the word of truth[18] as we seek to serve God in faithfulness to the Spirit-breathed pages of His Word.

There are many important differences between the Church, His body, and the churches of God. First amongst these is that there is only one Body which is being built and preserved by the Lord Jesus.[19] In contrast, there are many churches of God, in specific geographical localities, overseen and nourished by elders, to be a testimony for God on earth.[20]

Although the Body of Christ will never physically meet as one until it is gathered to meet the Lord in the air, churches of God meet together regularly, and individual believers move between churches, their reception for fellowship in divine service being commended by letters provided by their own assembly.[21] Secondly, the Church, His Body is associated with salvation and entered by baptism in the Holy Spirit, by which all are brought together into one without distinction on any ground.[22] Being in a church of God, however, requires baptism in water, and is associated with obedience in service, in which distinctions are drawn between masters and servants, men and women and their respective responsibilities in service.[23]

Finally, we discover that the unassailable nature of the Church, His Body, against which all the powers of evil are utterly without effect, is not shared by the church of God in local testimony. Neither the Church the Body itself,[24] nor the individual believer's place in it,[25] may be threatened by any act or omission. Yet, the place of an individual in a church of God, being based upon obedience, may be lost.[26] What is true of an individual can be true of an entire church of God, which may be susceptible to destruction on account of persecution[27] or a falling away from the truth.[28]

The Church Displayed in the Churches of God

Yet the drawing of this distinction between the Church, His Body and the churches of God is not to say that there is no synergy between them. It is not the purpose of His glorious Church to remain anonymous before the world. It is His Body, responding to the direction of the Head, working through believers on earth to display the majesty of His accomplished work. And it is in churches of God that the unity and vitality of His Church should be displayed – through local assemblies forming one community which, operating according to His pattern, display in microcosm the precious attributes of that great unseen Church.

As the Body of Christ as an entity is impervious to sinful influence, remaining as a matter of necessary fact 'subject to Christ',[29] the commandments embodied in the apostles' teaching, given to direct the behaviour of disciples, must have application in a forum where failure is a possibility.

It is by fulfilling these commandments, in unity towards each other and in obedience towards the Lord, that the beauty of the Body of Christ shall be displayed in a broken world. The unity of the Body will be seen by united teaching and practices amongst believers[30] who are united together in love;[31] and it will be established through saints using the gifts given to them by the Holy Spirit for the edification of the Body.[32]

"You are body of Christ", Paul told the Corinthians.[33] They were not, of course, the Body in all its fullness, but in character 'body of Christ, and members individually'. In churches of God today, we follow in their stead, seeking to give effect to the glorious unity and obedience of His Body in local, earthly testimony. As each church of God, and so the community as a whole, derives its unity from the Body, so each local church should reflect the wonderful attributes of that Body. The prize is well worth winning, for by doing so we shall *"come to the unity of the faith and of the knowledge of the Son of God, to a perfect man, to the measure of the stature of the fullness of Christ ... growing up in all things into Him who is the head – Christ".*[34]

[1] Matt.16:18; [2] See v.21; [3] Eph.1:22-23; Col.1:18; [4] Eph.3:4; [5] Eph.3:5; [6] Eph.5:30; [7] Eph.5:25; [8] 1 Cor.12:13; [9] Eph.3:10-11 ; [10] Eph.5:25,29,31-32; [11] Eph.5:27; Rev.19:7; [12] Acts 1:4-5; [13] Eph.1:23; [14] 1 Thess.4:15-17; [15] Rom.8:30; Eph.3:6; [16] Acts 7:38; [17] Acts 19:32,39; [18] 2 Tim.2:15; [19] Rom.12:5; Eph.4:4; Matt.16:18; Eph.5:23,29; 1:22-23; [20] 2 Thess.1:4; 1 Cor.1:2; Acts 20:17,28; 1 Thess.1:1,8; [21] Acts 18:27; Rom.16:1; 2 Cor.3:1; [22] Eph.3:6; 1 Cor.12:13; Gal.3:25-28; [23] Acts 2:41-42; 1 Tim.3:15; Col.3:18-4:11; 1 Cor.11:11,16; 14:33-35; [24] Matt.16:18; [25] John 10:28-29; 1 Cor.3:15; [26] 1 Cor.5:1-2,13; Matt.18:15-17; Titus 3:10; [27] Acts 8:1; Gal.1:13; [28] Rev.2:4-5; [29] Eph.5:24; [30] 1 Cor.4:17; [31] 1 Cor.12:21-26; [32] Eph.4:7-16; [33] 1 Cor.12:27; [34] Eph.4:13-15

Bible quotations from the NKJV

CHAPTER SIXTEEN: LIVING TO GOD'S PATTERN (DON WILLIAMSON)

'Kingdom living' seems to be a popular expression among many Christians today. I understand the thought behind it, but I'm also aware that life is full of clichés with little depth of thought about their meaning or consequences. You cannot live a life that is centred on yourself and the pleasures of this world and then have a token two-hour church experience and call that living to God's pattern. When the Lord Jesus explained to His disciples that He was the good Shepherd, He stressed, *"The thief comes only to steal and kill and destroy; I came that they may have life, and have it abundantly."*[1] Yes, we have life in Jesus because of His atoning work at Calvary, but the Lord wants us to have a fuller dimension of this life, and He calls it abundant!

Living as a Member of the Body of Christ

The apostle Paul gives us a truer insight as to the characteristics of the abundant life of believers with his words: *"Therefore if you have been raised up with Christ, keep seeking the things above, where Christ is, seated at the right hand of God. Set your mind on the things above, not on the things that are on earth. For you have died and your life is hidden with Christ in God."*[2] It would seem that the key is having a 'mindset' that we belong to Him and that it is no longer 'I' who live, but Christ living in me.

One thing we have to admit is that making a statement or quoting a line is much easier than actually **living** out the reality of these words. Perhaps it goes along with the saying, "I'd rather see a sermon than hear one any day!" Are you a walking sermon? The challenge of this way of life does not usually come from the outside, but from the inside. The people of Israel had this problem when it came to the pursuit of idols. They were not forced to go after the gods of the other nations; it appealed to their carnal nature and they set up dead idols, replacing the living God in the process.

We would never do that, would we? Here is what Paul says, "*Therefore consider the members of your earthly body as dead to immorality, impurity, passion, evil desire, and greed, which amounts to idolatry.*"[2] We cannot allow such desires to dominate our lives and at the same time hope to experience the fullness of Christ's abundant living. In a practical sense we are to put off things like anger, wrath, malice, slander, abusive speech and lying to one another. We need to replace those words with a focus on what our lives are to look like; "*So, as those who have been chosen of God, holy and beloved, put on a heart of compassion, kindness, humility, gentleness and patience, bearing with one another and forgiving each other.*"[4]

Understandable? Of course! Is it easy to put into practice? Maybe not. The Spirit of God, knowing our weaknesses, continues through Paul to instruct, *Beyond all these things put on love, which is the perfect bond of unity.*[5] Even the best of intentions needs the sustaining foundation of our love for the Lord Jesus. We are to be like Him as He was the perfect example of such living characteristics.

You will have noted the words '**put on**'. This suggests a determined action on our part to put into our daily reality a conduct that reflects the quality of those words. If you really want to see how you measure up, just apply these characteristics to your everyday actions and see how you do. The other key word in this area of living is '**let**'. "*Let the peace of Christ rule in your hearts, to which indeed you were called in one body; and be thankful. Let the word of Christ richly dwell within you, with all* *wisdom teaching and admonishing one another with psalms and hymns and spiritual songs, singing with thankfulness in your hearts to God."*[6]

Sometimes we 'let' the pressures of this life dictate what our life will consist of. The suggestion here is to yield what is already the Lord's – our life – and enjoy His peace, bask in His Word and at the end of the day be truly thankful. These things are to translate from words to deeds. Our living should be done in the name of the Lord Jesus, giving thanks through Him to God the Father.

Living Life in a Local Church of God

Guess what? Everything you have learned from living as a believer in the Church the Body, applies to your life in a Church of God.

I read an interesting quote the other day, 'When we get a grip on the reality of eternity and the superiority of the kingdom ... living from a kingdom point of view becomes a privilege, not a problem.'[7] First we should be eternally thankful for the fact that we are able to live a life after God's pattern. Without the new birth, the saving grace of the Lord Jesus, we would be like the walking dead. But in the power of a new life in Christ, we are able to *"proclaim the excellencies of Him who has called [us] out of darkness and into His marvelous light"*.[8] We can 'put on' Christ-like characteristics, letting Christ rule in us abundantly, according to His purpose. Does that sound like a two-hour token church experience? The richest expression of Christian living should be found in a church of God.

When Moses was instructed to go to Egypt and bring out the people of God, he was to say to Pharaoh, *"Thus says the Lord, the God of Israel, 'Let My people go that they may celebrate a feast to Me in the wilderness.'"*[9] The purpose of God was to have a people to worship Him and serve Him. Although there are many benefits for each of us individually living our lives according to His Word, the goal of Christ-like living is to fulfil that same purpose today as God set out in the beginning, and to see its expression in a collective service for God. Living the Christian life in a church of God should be exciting because it is a call according to His purpose. The church's experience when gathering is of those who have been 'living' and have now come to sing, praise and pray with thankful hearts. This should be our high watermark of service to the King! It is the collective expression of God's people in worship, witness and waiting.

In our waiting, we call upon the Lord in prayer, seeking His help while looking for His return. In our witness, we give an acknowledgement of the saving grace of the Lord Jesus and His claim on our lives, and in our worship, we bring our sacrifice of worshipful hearts for our Lord and Saviour Jesus Christ.

We face the same challenges to our 'living' collectively as we do individually. We often use 1 Corinthians 13 at a wedding service to show the true meaning of love. Paul is showing how we in the church should act towards each other as these gifts (of chs.12 & 14) are exercised in love. It is a description of the highest form of living stressing faith, hope and love, noting that the greatest of these is love![10]

How does your church reflect the characteristics of kingdom living? Remember, we are the church, so if we criticize, we are criticizing ourselves. Self examination is a good thing if it either confirms or leads to obedience to God's Word. Do we recognize God's pattern? Can we understand the words? Of course we can. Now we just have to do it! Let's experience kingdom living.

[1] John 10:10; [2] Col. 3:1-3; [3] Col. 3:5; [4] Col.3:12-13; [5] Col.3:14; [6] Col.3:15-16; [7] J. Stowell, Discovery Series: Kingdom Living; [8] 1 Pet.2:9; [9] Ex.5:1; [10] 1 Cor.13:13

Bible quotations from the NASB.

EPILOGUE

As you will have seen, there's no novelty to be found in these pages. In fact, rather the opposite. Some might indeed accuse us of setting back the cause of Christianity. To such a charge, should it arise, we would instantly plead guilty! It should be clear from the start of this volume that it has been our plain intention to see the cause of Christianity set back, not 100 years, but more than 1900 years - back to the doctrine that was current in Jerusalem with Peter and at Antioch with Paul.

The publishers of this book and of NT magazine, among whose pages these chapters first appeared as articles, take the description of early Christianity, as found in the New Testament Scriptures, to be equally prescriptive for today. A statement of beliefs drawn from these biblically reasoned core truths can be found at www.churchesofgod.info/church_of_god_beliefs/what-we-believe[1]

If, having read this book, you would like to enter into discussion on any aspect of its contents, then please use the 'contact us' facility on the aforementioned website.

---

1. http://www.churchesofgod.info/church_of_god_beliefs/what-we-believe

STUDY QUESTIONS

The Trinity

1. What do you think is the main reason why the doctrine of the Trinity is controversial?
2. How important is it in understanding human relationships for us to appreciate that God Himself exists in a relationship?
3. Is it helpful to our understanding of the Trinity to consider the revealed roles of each person as being particular focuses, but not exclusive ones?
4. How do you seek to develop your relationship with each member of the Trinity?

Eternally Secure Salvation

1. How does the fact of being baptised into the church which is the Body of Christ (1 Cor.12:13) help to provide assurance of eternal salvation? (see Matt.16:18)
2. If Heb.6:4-8 applies to eternally saved believers, from what do they fall away?
3. When will eternally saved believers appear before the Lord for judgement, and what will be the consequences? (see 1 Cor.3:12-15 and contrast with Rev.20:11-15)
4. Discuss the statement: "If I say that my salvation depends on my faithfulness, that means the sacrifice of Christ was inadequate to really save me."

Baptism of Believers

1. Which of the presented arguments is clearest for you

regarding a) baptism being intended to be by immersion; and
b) baptism not being necessary for salvation?

2. Does baptism symbolise our recognition that Christ died for
us or our recognition that we died with Him?

3. What practical difference has being baptised made in your
life?

"Do this until I come"

1. What similarities and differences can you find between the
observance of the former Sabbath and the Lord's Supper
today?

2. The 4th commandment is the only one not to be endorsed in
the New Testament, what instead gives substance to it in the
New Testament?

3. Describe in your own words the 3-fold rest from sin's slavery,
in service, and in the spiritual house. Reflect on how the
latter revelation is designed to promote a settled Christian
lifestyle.

4. What distinguishes remembering the Lord and His death
from the remembrance of other violent deaths?

The Lord's Return

1. What differences have you noted between the Lord's initial
return to the air for believers and the return of the Son of
Man to the earth?

2. Contrast and explain the descriptions of the 'Day of the
Lord' with the comfort promised believers when Christ
returns for them.

3. From 1 Corinthians 15, what changes in ourselves should we
expect when the Lord returns?

4. How should a belief in the imminent return of the Lord affect our approach to Christian service?

Spiritual Gifts

1. What is your spiritual gift (or gifts)? How did you become aware that God had given you this gift?
2. What do your 'significant others' say is your gift (ask your spouse, kids, parents, best friend, etc.)? Would others in your church identify your gift the same as you do?
3. How are you using it, that is, what is your ministry or area of service (or ministries, if more than one)? Give an example of God's effectiveness through you in your use of this gift?
4. What areas of gifts seem to be of greater need in your local church at the moment? Do the women have ample opportunity to exercise their gifts in suitable ministries? How can you ensure there is plenty of opportunity for them?
5. Give examples from Scripture of how the spiritual gifts we read about are characteristics of the Lord Jesus Christ who is the giver of the gifts.
6. In a smaller church there may be a need to be actively and enthusiastically engaged in service that does not fit my gifts. Give practical suggestions to help in making such service and its results more effective.

The Church and Churches of God

1. What are four different applications of the word 'church' found in the New Testament?

2. How many differences between the Church (Christ's Body) and local churches of God did you discover in these articles. Are there any more which you can add?

3. What characteristics of the Body should similarly characterise local churches of God?

4.Would you care to try to sum up in your own words some of the characteristics of the abundant life?

5.What ways have you found helpful in translating Christ-like characteristics which you have understood from Bible-reading all the way into your actual daily conduct?

6. Discuss, or personally reflect on, the connection between singing, praising and praying when we gather as a local church of God and our 'living' daily as members of the Body of Christ.

Did you love *Back to Basics: A Study of Core Bible Teaching and Practice*? Then you should read *Blood Most Precious - A Bible Study*[1] by EDWIN NEELY!

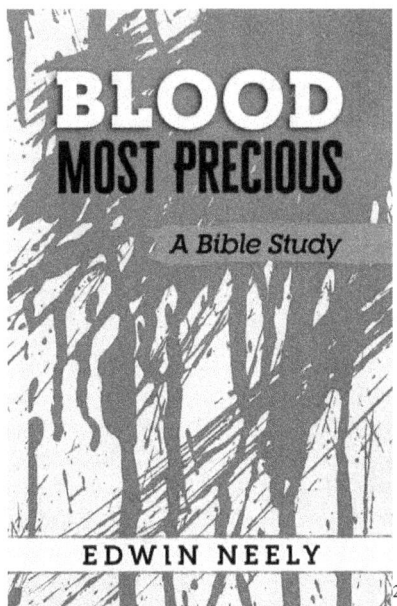

With no less than 375 Bible verses on the subject of blood, God definitely has something important to tell us about it. In this informative book, Edwin Neely explains its role and meaning under both the Old and New Covenants and its significance to us as Christians today – not just in our salvation, but in our service as well.

CHAPTER ONE: NON-SACRIFICIAL BLOOD

CHAPTER TWO: BLOOD IN NON-ALTAR SACRIFICES

CHAPTER THREE: THE SANCTITY OF THE BLOOD

CHAPTER FOUR: SPRINKLED BLOOD

CHAPTER FIVE: THE BLOOD OF THE SIN OFFERINGS

Also by Hayes Press

Bible Studies
Bible Studies 1990 - First Samuel
Bible Studies 1991 - The First Letter of Paul to the Corinthians
Bible Studies 1993 - Second Samuel
Bible Studies 1994 - The Establishment and Development of
Churches of God
Bible Studies 1995 - The Kings of Judah and Israel from Solomon to
Asa
Bible Studies 1992 - The Second Letter of Paul to the Corinthians

Needed Truth
Needed Truth 1888
Needed Truth 2001
Needed Truth 2002
Needed Truth 2003
Needed Truth 2004
Needed Truth 2005
Needed Truth 2006
Needed Truth 2007
Needed Truth 2008
Needed Truth 2009
Needed Truth 2010

Needed Truth 2011
Needed Truth 2012
Needed Truth 2015
Needed Truth 1888-1988: A Centenary Review of Major Themes

Standalone
The Road Through Calvary: 40 Devotional Readings
Lovers of God's House
Different Discipleship: Jesus' Sermon on the Mount
The House of God: Past, Present and Future
The Kingdom of God
Knowing God: His Names and Nature
Churches of God: Their Biblical Constitution and Functions
Four Books About Jesus
Collected Writings On ... Exploring Biblical Fellowship
Collected Writings On ... Exploring Biblical Hope
Collected Writings On ... The Cross of Christ
Builders for God
Collected Writings On ... Exploring Biblical Faithfulness
Collected Writings On ... Exploring Biblical Joy
Possessing the Land: Spiritual Lessons from Joshua
Collected Writings On ... Exploring Biblical Holiness
Collected Writings On ... Exploring Biblical Faith
Collected Writings On ... Exploring Biblical Love
These Three Remain...Exploring Biblical Faith, Hope and Love
The Teaching and Testimony of the Apostles
Pressure Points - Biblical Advice for 20 of Life's Biggest Challenges
More Than a Saviour: Exploring the Person and Work of Jesus
The Psalms: Volumes 1-4 Boxset
The Faith: Outlines of Scripture Doctrine
Key Doctrines of the Christian Gospel

Is There a Purpose to Life?
An Introduction to Bible Covenants
The Hidden Christ - Volume 2: Types and Shadows in Offerings and Sacrifices
The Hidden Christ Volume 1: Types and Shadows in the Old Testament
The Hidden Christ - Volume 3: Types and Shadows in Genesis
Heavenly Meanings - The Parables of Jesus
Fisherman to Follower: The Life and Teaching of Simon Peter
Called to Serve: Lessons from the Levites
Needed Truth 2017 Issue 1
The Breaking of the Bread: Its History, Its Observance, Its Meaning
Spiritual Revivals of the Bible
An Introduction to the Book of Hebrews
The Holy Spirit and the Believer
Exploring The Psalms: Volume 1 - Thoughts on Key Themes
Exploring The Psalms: Volume 2 - Exploring Key Elements
Exploring the Psalms: Volume 3 - Surveying Key Sections
The Psalms: Volume 4 - Savouring Choice Selections
Profiles of the Prophets
The Hidden Christ - Volumes 1-4 Box Set
The Hidden Christ - Volume 4: Types and Shadows in Israel's Tabernacle
Baptism - Its Meaning and Teaching
Conflict and Controversy in the Church of God in Corinth
In the Shadow of Calvary: A Bible Study of John 12-17
Moses: God's Deliverer
Sparkling Facets: Bible Names and Titles of Jesus
A Little Book About Being Christlike
Keys to Church Growth
From Shepherd Boy to Sovereign: The Life of David
Back to Basics: A Study of Core Bible Teaching and Practice
An Introduction to the Holy Spirit

Israel and the Church in Bible Prophecy
"Growth and Fruit" and Other Writings by John Drain
15 Hot Topics For Today's Christian
Needed Truth Volume 2 1889
Studies on the Return of Christ
Studies on the Resurrection of Christ
Needed Truth Volume 3 1890
The Nations of the Old Testament: Their Relationship with Israel and Bible Prophecy
The Message of the Minor Prophets
Insights from Isaiah
The Bible - Its Inspiration and Authority
Lessons from Ezra and Nehemiah
A Bible Study of God's Names For His People
Moses in One Hour
Abundant Christianity
Prayer in the New Testament

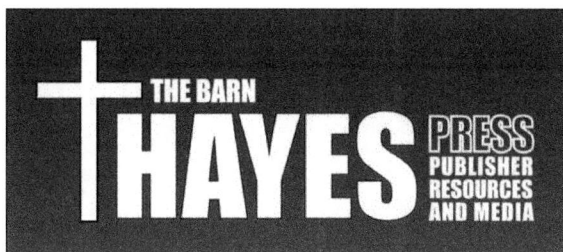

About the Publisher

Hayes Press (www.hayespress.org) is a registered charity in the United Kingdom, whose primary mission is to disseminate the Word of God, mainly through literature. It is one of the largest distributors of gospel tracts and leaflets in the United Kingdom, with over 100 titles and hundreds of thousands despatched annually. In addition to paperbacks and eBooks, Hayes Press also publishes Plus Eagles Wings, a fun and educational Bible magazine for children, and Golden Bells, a popular daily Bible reading calendar in wall or desk formats. Also available are over 100 Bibles in many different versions, shapes and sizes, Bible text posters and much more!